TWELVE GREAT BOOKS

JOSEPH PEARCE

Twelve Great Books

Going Deeper into Classic Literature

IGNATIUS PRESS   SAN FRANCISCO

Cover photograph and design by John Herreid
Inset images of William Shakespeare, Mary Shelley,
Charles Dickens, Oscar Wilde from public domain

Cover design by John Herreid

ISBN 978-1-62164-573-3 (PB)
ISBN 978-1-64229-214-5 (eBook)
Library of Congress Catalogue number 2022933992
Printed in the United States of America ∞

For Dale Ahlquist, Christopher Check,
William Fahey, and Daniel Kerr,
Fellow Troubadours and True Brothers

CONTENTS

ACKNOWLEDGMENTS

All the chapters in this book are modified versions of essays previously published in other publications.

The chapters on *Romeo and Juliet*, *Julius Caesar*, *Othello*, *Macbeth*, *Frankenstein*, *Wuthering Heights*, and *The Picture of Dorian Gray* were previously published as the introductions to the Ignatius Critical Editions of these respective works.

The chapter on St. Augustine's *Confessions* was first published as the introduction to the Noll Library edition of *Confessions* published by Our Sunday Visitor (2018).

The chapter on *A Christmas Carol* was first published as "Holy Ghosts and the Spirit of Christmas" in *Chronicles* 38, no. 12 (December 2014).

The chapter on *The Man Who Was Thursday* was first published as "Questioning Chesterton's Own Judgment of *The Man Who Was Thursday*" in *The Imaginative Conservative*, May 28, 2020.

The chapter on *The Power and the Glory* was originally published in *The Roman Catholic Arts Review* 1 (2010).

The chapter on *Brideshead Revisited* was first published as "Revisiting Brideshead" in *Chronicles* 39, no. 6 (June 2015).

The appendix on *Sir Thomas More* was first published as the introduction to the first Spanish language edition of the play (Madrid: Ediciones Rialp, 2012). Its first publication in English was by *The Latin Mass: The Journal of Catholic Culture and Tradition* 22, no. 2 (Summer 2013).

INTRODUCTION TO THE
GREAT BOOKS OF CIVILIZATION

In introducing anything, it is always wise to begin by defining our terms. What are the Great Books? What is civilization? We'll begin with the definition of the latter, and with the refutation of common misperceptions of what constitutes civilization.[1]

Civilization is not merely the set of customs adopted by a specific people, nor is it defined by the level of complexity within a society. Customs can be dreadfully uncivilized and complex cultures can be truly evil. To speak, for instance, of "Nazi civilization" or "Soviet civilization" is to utter an oxymoron. Put plainly and unequivocally, individuals and societies that are not civilized cannot be part of civilization. In other words, civilization is rooted in morality, and anything rooted in morality is *ipso facto* rooted in philosophy and theology. Thus, putting aside these incorrect definitions, and these false and fashionable notions of civilization, the thing itself can be defined as the harmony that arises from the ordering of the life of an individual (or a society) in accordance with his (or its) objective place within the cosmos. Note the word "objective". It is crucial. Civilization, as an objective entity, is

---

[1] This definition of civilization transcends the common definition rooted in the Latin *civilis*, meaning merely "citizen", and has its root in the Augustinian notion that true citizenship, i.e., true civilization, is reserved for those who owe their allegiance to the *civitas Dei* (city of God) as opposed to the *civitas Terrena* (city of Man).

not dependent on who we *think* we are, and what we *think* our place is within the wider scheme of things; it is dependent on who we *really* are, whether we like it or not (or know it or not), and where we belong in an objectively ordered *reality*. If civilization is real, it cannot be subject to what we think of it because reality is not subject to what we think of it. The subjectivism (relativism) that denies this foundational fact is inherently deficient in any true awareness of the place of an individual or society within an objectively real cosmos and is *ipso facto* uncivilized.

Having rejected the uncivilized folly of subjectivism, we come to understand that civilization is not subject to our own thoughts or feelings but to the truth beyond ourselves. Since this is so, we cannot know what is civilized *until* we know what is true. The best place to find the truth and to discover the answers to the riddle of man's *being* and *purpose* is in the perennial teaching of Christianity that we are made by God to show forth His goodness and to share eternally in His happiness in heaven. In order to gain this heavenly happiness, we must know, love, and serve God in this world. We are creatures, made by the Creator, and His will is that we should find eternal joy by knowing, loving, and serving Him. This is who we are and where we fit into the cosmos. And this is the very key to civilization. Knowing this fundamental truth and living in obedience to the responsibilities it places upon us *makes* us civilized; failing to know the truth and thereby failing to order our lives in accordance with our responsibilities makes us uncivilized.

Implicit in the Christian understanding of man's being and purpose is the fact that the human person is *homo viator*, a pilgrim or wayfarer who journeys through mortal life with eternal life always in mind. And yet the great tragedy of our own deplorable epoch is that modern man does not see himself as *homo viator*. "The modern man," wrote G. K. Chesterton, "is more like a traveller who has forgotten the name of his destination, and has to go back whence he came, even to find out where he is going."[2] *Pace* Chesterton, modern man has not only forgotten the name of his destination; he has even forgotten that he has a destination. He does not know that he is a traveler. He is unaware that he is on a journey or that he has anywhere to go. He is not *homo viator*, nor is he *homo sapiens*, in the sense that he does not know the difference between sapience and techne, or between wisdom and knowledge; he is *homo superbus*, a pathetic creature trapped within the confines of his own self-constructed "self". Making himself the sole arbiter of all "truth" and "morality", he has shrunk the cosmos to the size of his own ego. He is, in fact, such a pathetic creature that he does not even know that he is a creature, in the sense that he does not know or arrogantly denies that he has been created. He has disowned and dethroned God and has made himself the de facto god of his own creation.

Homo superbus believes that man's essential purpose is to love and serve himself. He is motivated by the sin of superbia, the pride that animated Satan's rebellion, and Adam and Eve's. His self-centered motto is Satan's *non serviam* (I will not serve), or Polonius' advice to his son in William Shakespeare's *Hamlet*: "This above all—to thine own self be true" (1.3.78).[3] Polonius, as *homo superbus* personified, believes that there is no truth beyond the self and therefore nothing to be true to except the self. It is the reductionism of Descartes' *cogito ergo sum* (I think, therefore I am)

---

[2] Michael Ffinch, *G. K. Chesterton: A Biography* (San Francisco: Harper & Row, 1986), p. 258.

[3] *Hamlet*, ed. Joseph Pearce, Ignatius Critical Editions (San Francisco: Ignatius Press, 2008). Text references are to act, scene, and line.

metamorphosed into the *reductio ad absurdum* of "I think, therefore everything else is (or isn't)." Countering this Cartesian fundamentalism, Etienne Gilson, following the philosophy of his master, Thomas Aquinas, gives the alternative view of man as one who reflects and partakes in the goodness, truth, and beauty of God:

> Man is not a mind that thinks, but a being who knows other beings as true, who loves them as good, and who enjoys them as beautiful. For all that which is, down to the humblest form of existence, exhibits the inseparable privileges of being, which is truth, goodness and beauty.[4]

In conclusion, and in a nutshell, civilization can be defined as the fruits of the works of *homo viator*; whereas its opposite, barbarism, can be defined as the bitter fruits of the works of *homo superbus*. The civilized man is inspired in all that he does by the desire to serve God and his neighbor; the barbarian is inspired by his desire to please himself. If it be argued that history is full of virtuous barbarians, or noble savages, who do not conform to the philosophy and behavior of *homo superbus*, the response would be that such "barbarians", insofar as they exhibit the characteristics of *homo viator*, albeit unknowingly, are thereby not "barbarians" at all! On the other hand, cynics and relativists are always barbarians, even if their sophistry and eloquence, and their airs and graces, give them the outward appearance of civilization.

This understanding of civilization necessitates a denial of the Enlightenment fallacy that man is progressing from a primitive barbaric past to a sophisticated civilized future. On the contrary, man is always oscillating between the two

---

[4] Etienne Gilson, *The Unity of Philosophical Experience* (New York: Charles Scribner's Sons, 1937), p. 317.

poles of his very nature. He is either falling into the folly of the idolatrous love of himself above all others (the barbarism of *homo superbus*), or he is edified by his selfless love for the other (the civilization of *homo viator*). Since this oscillation between sin and virtue is to be found in the heart of every man, it is also to be found at the heart of every age in history. In this sense, there is no golden age in the past. Where we find saints we always find sinners. Yet the absence of a golden age does not mean that some ages were not better than others. Each age is characterized by the dominant ideas that animated and motivated its actions, its struggles, its politics, and its art. These ideas leave their indelible mark upon the age, enabling us to see the broad sweep of civilization and barbarism across the centuries.

The history of the West can be divided into three broad ages of man: the pre-Christian or pagan age; the age of Christendom; and the age of disenchantment.

In the pre-Christian age, artists and philosophers examined the struggle between *homo viator* and *homo superbus*, seeing the former as virtuous and the latter as vicious. In the age of Christendom, the affirmation of *homo viator* and the condemnation of *homo superbus* was subsumed within the very fabric of culture as a societal manifestation of the inner struggle in each individual's heart and conscience. It was seen as being incumbent upon all men to overcome the temptations of *homo superbus* (the barbarian within ourselves) and to become perfect examples of *homo viator* (the saint as the epitome of the civilized man). In this sense, the age of Christendom corresponds to the finest flowering of civilization. It is an age in which the union of faith and reason, as made manifest in the unity of theology and philosophy, meant that sanity was seen as being synonymous with sanctity. Being civilized (holy) in the city of Man was the means of attaining the perfect civilization of heaven, the city of God. In its theology, its philosophy, its painting, its architecture, its sculpture, its music, its literature, the age of Christendom aspired toward the integrated harmony, the wholeness and oneness, of its Founder.

The age of disenchantment is characterized by a progressive fragmentation of thought in which the wholeness and holiness of Christendom is abandoned. From the decay of the Christian humanism and neo-classicism of the Renaissance and its coming of age in the pride of the superciliously self-named Enlightenment, the age of disenchantment can now be seen to be unraveling in the self-defeating nonsense of its own nihilistic deconstruction.

It is important to remember that disenchantment has not replaced Christendom, in the sense that it has somehow eclipsed or extinguished the age that preceded it. On the contrary, the presence of Christendom within a disenchanted culture can be seen in the magic or miracle of reenchantment. The works of Shakespeare, John Dryden, Samuel Johnson, William Blake, Samuel Coleridge, William Wordsworth, Sir Walter Scott, Charles Dickens, Fyodor Dostoevsky, G.K. Chesterton, C.S. Lewis, J.R.R. Tolkien, Evelyn Waugh, and T.S. Eliot, to name but an illustrious few, are inspired by a rejection of disenchantment and a desire for reenchantment. And what is true of literature is true of painting (the Pre-Raphaelites), architecture (the Gothic Revival), and music (Anton Bruckner, Gustav Mahler, Felix Mendelssohn, Olivier Messiaen, Arvo Pärt, and others). This disillusionment with disenchantment represents a healthy reaction against the cold mechanism of the materialist or the meaningless mess of the nihilist; it is an awakening to the enchantment of reality, perceiving it as a miraculous harmony of being, a song, a Great Music. In our own age, the struggle between *homo superbus* and *homo viator* manifests itself in disenchantment and reenchantment.

Having defined what is meant by civilization, let's proceed to a definition of what constitutes a "Great Book" in the light of our understanding of civilization. Books can be "great" in two distinct and crucially different ways. They can be "great" objectively, in what they *are*, and they can be "great" subjectively, in what they have *done*. Dante's *Divine Comedy* is an objectively "great" book, perhaps objectively the greatest book, in its literary brilliance as a poem and in its sublime exposition of the supernatural destiny of *homo viator* in the light of the theology and philosophy of Christendom. On the other hand, James Joyce's 1916 *Portrait of the Artist as a Young Man* is a "great" book subjectively in the sense that it is a work of literature that has impacted the culture of the past century to a great degree. It is, however, a eulogy in defense of *homo superbus* and is, as such, an uncivilized work, lacking goodness, truth, and beauty. It is, therefore, not an objectively "great" book, which is defined by the degree to which it is civilized, but a subjectively "great" book, which is defined by the degree to which it has done important things to the culture. We should remind ourselves that "important" is emphatically not synonymous with "good". Evil is important, in the sense that we do it or ignore it at our peril, but it is not good. The Third Reich is one of the most important chapters in twentieth-century history but not because Hitler's regime was good. Similarly, we should remind ourselves that "culture" is not synonymous with "good". James Joyce's book is a significant work of *culture* while, at the same time, being profoundly *uncivilized*, and therefore harmful to all that is good, true, and beautiful. The obvious analogy is with those other "cultures" that appear in nature. Biological cultures can bring both health and death, and just as it is perilous to the body to see no difference between penicillin and E. coli, so it is perilous to the soul to see no difference between good culture (civilization) and bad culture (barbarism). It is, therefore, important to remember that cultures can be barbaric. The culture of death in the Third Reich led to millions dying in concentration camps; the culture of death in the Soviet Union led to millions dying in the Gulag Archipelago; and the culture of death in today's institutionalized hedonism is killing millions of unborn children in abortion mills. These are all barbaric cultures ruled over by cultured barbarians. Let's never fall into the trap of believing that something is good or civilized merely because it is cultured.

Now that we have defined our terms, we should be able to distinguish those books that are genuinely great or civilized, in the objective sense in which they mirror man's true image as *homo viator*, from those that are only great in the subjective sense in which they have had a great and important impact upon history through their reflection of the beliefs of *homo superbus*, man's self-deceptive and destructive alter ego. The former are towering testaments to the cooperation of the gifted with the Giver of the gift; high places from which we can survey reality more clearly; edifices that edify. The latter are towering testaments to human pride; high places covered with clouds that prevent us from seeing anything but ourselves; edifices from which we fall. The former are great in the sense that they shine forth the sacred heart of truth, goodness, and beauty. The latter are great in the sense that they grate the truth, shredding its surface without ever reaching or touching its core.

Let's end this brief introduction to the Great Books by taking a voyage through the history of Western civilization, considering which books are truly great from those that are great truth-graters.

Commencing our odyssey in the pre-Christian or pagan age, we can declare that Homer deserves a place among the truly great for his depiction of the goodness of *homo viator* and the follies of *homo superbus*. In the opening lines of the *Iliad*, the great poet unlocks the morality of the epic drama that is about to unfold by asking for the grace of the gods to show the devastation caused by the prideful anger of Achilles and how the will of God (Zeus) is accomplished in the unfolding of events. The pride of *homo superbus* represented primarily by the actions of Agamemnon, Achilles, and Paris is punished in accordance with the overriding will of Zeus. It is also surely significant that the epic ends with praises being sung for the fallen hero, Hector, and not for his conqueror, Achilles. It might also be argued that Homer presents us with the key to understanding his own moral position in the metaphors of reconciliation offered in the epic's penultimate book, in which magnanimity and forgiveness triumph over prideful vengeance. This reading of the *Iliad* may militate against the notion of "pagan heroism" advocated by the neo-classicism of the Enlightenment, but it is in complete harmony with the insistence of J. R. R. Tolkien and C. S. Lewis that the pagan myths contain splintered fragments of the one true light that comes from God. The neo-classicists of the disenchantment were attracted to paganism as a means of escaping from the constraints of Christian moral theology, and they read Homer in accordance with this prejudiced desire for moral iconoclasm. For Tolkien and Lewis, however, the pagans were looking for the light that would eventually be revealed in Christ and were assisted in that quest by the grace of the God that they did not know. As Lewis tells us in *The Pilgrim's Regress*, God inspired the pagans with pictures (myths) because they had forgotten how to read. Homer's Muse was, therefore, a grace that he only partially comprehended, but which he served with the utmost fidelity, with triumphant results.

The same triumphant results were achieved in Homer's other great epic, the *Odyssey*, in which the hero is literally *homo viator* making sacrifices in order to get home. As with the protagonists in the *Iliad*, Odysseus is punished when he forgets his calling as *homo viator* and succumbs to the temptation of *homo superbus*. His boastfulness after the blinding of Polyphemus brings down the curse that destroys his men and delays his own homecoming. If he had been content in decorous humility to remain "Nobody", he would have arrived home expeditiously with his men and ships unharmed; in succumbing to the pride of exalting himself, he is humbled by the punishment of the gods. The *Odyssey*'s subplot also revolves around the theme of man as *homo viator* in the growth to physical and emotional maturity of Telemachos. The journey of Odysseus' son from the inadequacy of boyhood to the fullness of manhood is *homo viator*'s rite of passage. For Homer, the true purpose of man is not the static self-absorption of *homo superbus* but the dynamic progress of *homo viator* toward the goal that is his destiny. Finally, for good measure, Homer gives us in the figure of the self-sacrificially circumspect Penelope, the first icon of idealized femininity, a paragon of womanly virtue worthy of the company of Dante's Beatrice and Shakespeare's Cordelia.

In Aeschylus' *Oresteia* and Sophocles' *Oedipus Cycle*, we see the first buds of a new springtime of philosophical questioning prophesying the full flowering of Greek philosophy under Socrates, Plato, and Aristotle. Aeschylus asks fundamental questions about the nature of justice and the role of the divine in breaking the endless cycle of vengeance inherent in human law; Sophocles shows us Oedipus as *homo viator*, a Job-like figure, more sinned against than sinning, who grows in wisdom and virtue through the experience of suffering until, ripened into sanctity, he warrants a mystical assumption into heaven at the end of his life. In *Antigone*, Sophocles has given us a timeless work of literature and political philosophy, providing profound insights into the relationship between religion and the state, and between natural law and human law. Antigone's adherence to the rights of religion over those of the state, and her insistence that the natural law cannot be contradicted by human law, is rooted in her understanding of herself as *homo viator*, whose life on earth is merely a transient phase leading ultimately to the life of eternity.

The fundamental questions asked by the giants of Greek literature were taken up by the great Greek philosophers, and it has been said that all subsequent philosophy is but footnotes on the ideas enunciated by the Greeks. It is indeed one of the great tragedies of the age of disenchantment that the footnotes to Plato and Aristotle are being written by those who have not understood the text upon which they are commenting. For the age of Christendom, however, the Greeks were allies upon whom the foundations of Christian philosophy were laid. Augustine, Thomas Aquinas, and the great Christian philosophers were hugely indebted to Plato and Aristotle and used the ideas of their illustrious forebears to forge the impregnable armor of *fides et ratio* with which Christendom has withstood the claims of heretical theology and false philosophy.

The Great Books of early Christendom, such as Augustine's *Confessions* and *City of God* and Boethius' *Consolation of Philosophy*, bear the hallmark of Greek philosophy, and the highest philosophical achievement of the whole of Christendom, the *Summa* of Thomas Aquinas, can be seen as a dialogue with, and a perfection of, Aristotelianism. Dante's *Divine Comedy*, Christendom's highest work of literary art, is a poetic commentary on Aquinas' *Summa*, in which Dante, as a character within the work representing

Everyman or *homo viator* personified, goes on a journey from the dark wood of sin to the heights of heaven. As the *Divine Comedy* unfolds, the dynamism of *homo viator* ascending Mount Purgatory through the motivating power of penance, and the overflowing joy of the souls who have reached their true home in paradise, is contrasted with the stagnant stasis of *homo superba* stuck forever in the flames of his own egocentric passion. It is indeed ironic, and tragi-comic, that the age of disenchantment only reads the *Inferno*, considering it better than *Purgatory* or *Paradise*. Clearly the age of *homo superba* finds itself stuck where it evidently belongs!

In Chaucer's *Canterbury Tales*, one of the truly Great Books of Christendom, all of the characters are on a journey in the literal or physical sense of being on a pilgrimage to Canterbury, but only some of them are on the deeper pilgrimage that leads, via Canterbury, to heaven. The work serves to illustrate the genuine pilgrim (*homo viator*) from the hypocrites (*homo superba*) who are only along for the ride. As such, Chaucer's *Tales* can be seen as a dialogue between *homo viator* and *homo superba*, in which the latter is exposed as being hypocritical through Chaucer's ingenious use of allegory and irony. In this, as in all the works of Christendom, *homo viator* is the hero and *homo superba* the villain.

Once we move into the age of disenchantment, we see the schism between the new spirit of skeptical humanism (*homo superba*) and the reaction against it in the form of tradition-oriented works of reenchantment, which can be seen as *homo viator*'s riposte to the attack upon him. Thus, for instance, Thomas More's *Utopia* and the works of Shakespeare can be seen as ripostes to the new humanism of Machiavelli and to the rise of anti-clerical secularism in England.

The disenchantment of Puritan fundamentalism that sought to remove song, ritual, and art from religious worship was countered by the reenchantment of the Metaphysical poets and, later, by Dryden in poems such as *Religio Laici* and *The Hind and the Panther*. The disenchantment of eighteenth-century rationalism was countered by the conservative reenchantment of Samuel Johnson, the radical conservatism of William Cobbett, and the Romanticism of Blake, Wordsworth, Coleridge, and Sir Walter Scott. The disenchantment with the past inherent in the rampant modernism of the industrial revolution was countered by the reenchantment of Romanticism and neo-medievalism, the latter of which spawned the Gothic Revival, the Pre-Raphaelites, and the Oxford Movement. The disenchantment of the dark Romanticism of Byron and Shelley led to the reenchanted darkness of the Decadents, such as Charles Baudelaire, Paul Verlaine, Joris-Karl Huysmans, and Oscar Wilde, all of whom became converts to Catholicism. The cold disenchantment of Victorian utilitarianism was confuted by the enchanted world of Dickens and his enchanting characters. The nihilistic disenchantment and despair of the twentieth century has inspired the reenchanted beauty of the works of Chesterton, Tolkien, Lewis, Waugh, and Eliot. For all its bombast and bluster, the forces of disenchantment in our own time have not produced works as magnificent and popularly successful as *Brideshead Revisited*, *The Lord of the Rings*, or *The Chronicles of Narnia*. There is no poetry of disenchantment in the twentieth century to match the beauty of T. S. Eliot's *Four Quartets*, and the greatest poem of disillusionment in the past century, Eliot's "The Waste Land", is inspired by a profound disillusionment with disillusionment!

Disenchanted with disenchantment, these multifarious authors and poets serve to illustrate that Great Books are still being written in spite of the prevailing spirit of gloom imposed upon our times by the destructive power of *homo superbus* and the deplorable zeitgeist that is his inheritance.

His inheritance is not our inheritance. The Great Books are our inheritance. They are the inheritance of all of us, or all of us who want them. In reading the Great Books, we find ourselves in the presence of Great Minds thinking about Great Things. We find ourselves in the presence of almost three thousand years of genius. We find ourselves in the company of the *illustrissimi* of civilization. In what better company could we possibly hope to spend our time? This side of the grave, there is no better company. The better company, the best possible company, awaits *homo viator* after his temporal journey is over. In the meantime, and we live in mean times, the Great Books are good companions for the journey and excellent guides. Like the *lembas* (journey bread) that sustained Frodo and Sam on their journey through Mordor to Mount Doom, the Great Books are manna for the mind and food for the soul.

Chapter One

St. Augustine's *Confessions*

If any single book can claim to be the quintessential Christian classic, it must be St. Augustine's *Confessions*. There are other claimants to the accolade, to be sure. One thinks perhaps of Augustine's other masterpiece, *The City of God*, or the *Summa Theologica* of St. Thomas Aquinas, or possibly, if one is seeking lighter fare, *The Imitation of Christ* by Thomas à Kempis or St. Francis de Sales' *Introduction to the Devout Life*. And if we are to include works of literature, as well as works of nonfiction, we might suggest *The Divine Comedy* or even, at a heterodox stretch, *Paradise Lost*. And what of modern Christian classics, such as Chesterton's *Orthodoxy* and *The Everlasting Man*, or C. S. Lewis' *Mere Christianity* and *The Screwtape Letters*? All of these books can claim to be Christian classics (though Milton's non-Trinitarian theology stretches the definition of "Christianity" to breaking point), and they are all eminently worth taking the time to read. And yet if we could only read one of these books, or if we were allowed to take just one of them with us to the proverbial desert island, could we really bear to part with *The Confessions*? Could we contemplate being apart from it? Could we really see ourselves departing to the place of solitude without it?

Apart from being a purely Christian classic, there is no doubt that *The Confessions* is one of the Great Books, those seminal tomes, both Christian and non-Christian, which form the very foundation of the Western canon and which represent, collectively, the *illustrissimi* and *eminenti* of all published works. It sits comfortably beside the works of Plato, Aristotle, and Aquinas. It is of their company. And yet there's something about *The Confessions* that puts it in a class of its own, even in such elite company. It is unique. It is unlike all the other Great Books. It contains philosophy, and yet it is unlike any other philosophical work. It grapples with questions of theology but not in the same way that theologians normally do their grappling. It is autobiographical, but it is not merely an autobiography; it is, rather, the very archetype of all autobiography, the first and the best of the genre, the standard by which all autobiography is measured. Furthermore, and this is perhaps the ultimate test, it is sublimely *accessible* and perennially *applicable*. It speaks to our age, as it spoke to Augustine's own age, because it speaks to all ages. It cuts through the cant of all the intellectual fads and fashions, those *accidents* of history (philosophically speaking) which do not partake of those truths which are truly *essential* to our understanding of ourselves, of each other, and of our place in the cosmos.

Augustine is accessible and applicable because he is one of us. He struggles with the same temptations with which we struggle, and he succumbs to them as we do. He falls and does not always get up again, preferring to wallow in the gutter with his lusts and his illicit appetites. And yet, like us, he is restless until he rests in the truth, which can be found only in Christ and the Church He founded.

Unlike the other great philosophers, Augustine doesn't seek in *The Confessions* to show us the truth purely objectively, by setting out the abstract concepts and proving his point with dispassionate and logical reasoning. He seeks to show us the objective truth through his subjective engagement with it and by the consequences of his failure to engage with it. And yet this *subjective* approach has *objective* power because, in putting himself in his own shoes, he is putting himself in our shoes also. In describing himself, he is simultaneously describing us. He and we are one. We share the same humanity with all that it entails. In seeing him and his struggles, we see ourselves and our own struggles, and the struggles of each other.

The perennial applicability of *The Confessions* was illustrated potently by Fr. David Meconi in his whimsical composition of a letter that he imagines the seventeen-year-old Augustine might have written to his long-suffering mother (St. Monica) from college. "Mom, I wish you could meet my new girlfriend," Augustine writes. "We may come from very different places, but we have taught each other some important lessons. We have been staying together for a year or so now, and want you to know that you are soon going to meet your grandson!"[1] In presenting the autobiographical facts of Augustine's life in the twenty-first-century idiom, Fr. Meconi allows us to see something of enduring relevance in the life Augustine lived and the life lessons he learned, albeit that he lived his life sixteen hundred years ago. Perhaps we were the college student who decided to "shack-up" with a girlfriend. Perhaps we got a girlfriend pregnant. Or perhaps we were the mother whose college-age son or daughter dropped the bombshell about their lifestyle choices. *Plus ça change, plus c'est la même chose!* (The more things change, the more they remain the same!)

[1] David Vincent Meconi, S.J., in his Introduction to *The Confessions*, by Saint Augustine of Hippo, trans. Maria Boulding, O.S.B., ed. David Vincent Meconi, S.J., Ignatius Critical Editions, ed. Joseph Pearce (San Francisco: Ignatius Press, 2012), p. vii.

In the same letter, Fr. Meconi imagines Augustine telling his mother that he intends to switch majors from law
to philosophy because he had read some good books and
wonders whether perhaps there is something or someone
that attracts and moves people toward the truth. "But I
don't know," he adds, "living without insisting on truth
is a lot easier."[2] For the young Augustine in the fourth
century as for the young college student in the twenty-
first century, relativism is a pragmatic choice, a path of
least intellectual resistance that enables him to indulge his
lower appetites without asking too many awkward moral
questions. *Plus ça change, . . .*

The next bombshell that Fr. Meconi imagines the teenage Augustine dropping on his devout Catholic mother
is also all too familiar. He informs her that he has stopped
going to the Catholic Church and is now a follower of
a new age dualistic sect, which in his day was known as
Manichaeism but in our day goes by other names. *Plus ça
change, . . .*

Augustine is "a perennial figure", writes Fr. Meconi,
"no different from most young people of each age".[3] Like
young people of all ages Augustine has a "restless heart",[4]
seeking pleasure in all the wrong places. He is different
from some, though mercifully not all, in that he finally
found rest and real happiness in the only place it can truly
be found: in the presence of God.

Like Fr. Meconi, I have also perceived a striking similarity between my own "restless heart", as a young man, and
the restless heart of Augustine, a similarity that is discussed
in my own conversion story, my own "confessions", *Race*

---

[2] Ibid.
[3] Ibid., p. viii.
[4] Ibid.

with the Devil: My Journey from Racial Hatred to Rational Love.[5] I will quote the whole passage that connects my own twentieth-century childhood with Augustine's childhood sixteen hundred years earlier, because it serves as an evocative example of the accessibility and applicability of *The Confessions*:

> Summer and autumn was scrumping season, during which we descended like a band of brigands or pirates on the neighbouring orchards, pillaging plums, pears, apples and strawberries as each fruit ripened, or often before they ripened. The ensuing stomach aches were attributed by my mother to the gluttonous quantity of fruit that we had consumed or the fact that it was not yet ripe, but I fancy that it may also have been due to the ingestion of the noxious chemicals that farmers by the 1960s were beginning to spray on their crops. Needless to say, we ate as we plucked and never thought about washing the fruit before consuming it.
>
> It is odd that we gained such pleasure from this theft of the farmers' crops. There was a thrill to be had in climbing the fence into the orchard, in trespassing on someone else's property, in the risk of being caught, in the plucking of the forbidden fruit, in the eating of it. I am reminded in adulthood of St. Augustine's conscience-driven memory, recounted in his *Confessions*, of his own scrumping expedition as a child. He recalls "a pear tree laden with fruit" near his childhood home and the night-time raids that he and his friends made upon it. "We took enormous quantities, not to feast on ourselves but perhaps to throw to the pigs; we did eat a few, but that was not our motive: we derived pleasure from the deed simply because it was forbidden."[6]

[5] Joseph Pearce, *Race with the Devil: My Journey from Racial Hatred to Rational Love* (Charlotte, N.C.: Saint Benedict Press, 2013).

[6] Pearce, *Race with the Devil*, pp. 12–13. Quote from the *Confessions* is from the Ignatius Critical Editions, p. 41.

St. Augustine's timely and timeless musings on the presence of concupiscence in the heart of youth serves to remind us that the innocence of childhood is not synonymous with the absence of sin. The arcadia in which we resided was not Eden. Although we lived in blissful ignorance of the nature and magnitude of the adult sins that surrounded us, we could indulge in our own childish forms of them and did so with devilish delight. As sons of Adam, we were willing apprentices in the antediluvian art of sin and became more adept in our practice of it as we got older but no wiser. It is for this reason that fairytales play such a healthy part in childhood. It is necessary for children to know that fairyland contains dragons, giants, and wicked witches, because the real world contains grown-up versions of these evil creatures of which children need to have at least an inkling.

Apart from the parallels between my own "restless" journey through the dark wood of sin and error, and that of Augustine's, I am aware that my own telling of the story is in some senses a retelling of the story that he had already told so much better. All such "confessions", all such conversion stories, are merely types of Augustine's archetype. Even John Henry Newman's 1864 *Apologia pro Vita Sua*,[7] perhaps the greatest autobiographical conversion memoir ever written, except for *The Confessions* itself, is but a formal reflection of Augustine's original "apologia". The eminent Victorian's apology for his life merely follows in Augustine's venerable footsteps and the confessional trail he had already blazed. The same could be said of R. H. Benson's 1913 *Confessions of a Convert*[8] and Msgr. Ronald

[7] See John Henry Newman, *Apologia pro Vita Sua*, ed. Ian Ker (London: Penguin Books, 1994).

[8] Robert Hugh Benson, *Confessions of a Convert* (Plano, Tex.: Bridegroom Press, 1913).

Knox's 1918 *A Spiritual Aeneid.*[9] All great confessional literature and all great conversion stories take their lead and their cue from Augustine's magisterial original. *Plus ça change, . . .*

This somewhat rambling preamble to Augustine's *Confessions* has barely scratched the surface of all that *The Confessions* has to offer. It has not discussed Augustine's philosophical and theological engagement with the Neoplatonists, or with the Manichaeans; nor has it discussed his rational and psychological grappling with grief and the meaning of mortality; nor has it so much as mentioned Augustine's relationship with his mentor, St. Ambrose, a neglectful fact that is truly a sin of omission. And yet, when all is said and done, the most potent and important reason for anyone reading *The Confessions* is the insights it gives into one of the greatest minds in history. Why would we not want to spend time in the company of one of the greatest men who ever lived and in the presence of one of the greatest minds that God has ever loved?

---

[9] Ronald Knox, *A Spiritual Aeneid* (New York: Longmans, Green, 1918).

Chapter Two

Romeo and Juliet

As with so many of Shakespeare's plays, the exact date of *Romeo and Juliet*'s composition is shrouded in mystery and is the cause of much scholarly argument and disagreement. When it appeared in print for the first time, in 1597, the title page referred to its being performed "with great applause" by Lord Hunsdon's Men. Since Shakespeare's acting troupe was known as Lord Hunsdon's Men between only July 1596 and March 1597, it is assumed, logically enough, that the play must have been written in 1595 or 1596. Some scholars believe, however, that it was written as early as 1591, arguing that the Nurse's remark, "'Tis since the earthquake now eleven years" (1.3.23),[1] constitutes a clear allusion to the London earthquake of 1580. Countering such a suggestion, advocates of the later date refer to William Covell's *Polimanteia*, a work with which they presume Shakespeare was aware, that alludes to an earthquake of 1584.

Much less controversial than the dating of the play is the principal source upon which it is based. All critics seem to agree that the main wellspring of Shakespeare's inspiration for *Romeo and Juliet* was Arthur Brooke's long poem, *The Tragicall Historye of Romeus and Juliet*, published in 1562.

---

[1] *Romeo and Juliet*, ed. Joseph Pearce, Ignatius Critical Editions (San Francisco: Ignatius Press, 2011). Text references are to act, scene, and line.

Although Brooke was himself indebted to a tradition of romantic tragedies emanating from the Italian Renaissance, it seems that the essential ingredients of Shakespeare's play are taken from Brooke's poem. Since Shakespeare's *modus operandi* often involved the confuting of his sources, correcting their biases into modes of expression more conducive to his own beliefs, it is worth looking at Brooke's poem in order to see what it is that Shakespeare does to it. Before doing so, we should remind ourselves that this "correcting" of his sources is something with which Shakespeare would remain preoccupied.

Shortly before embarking upon the writing of *Romeo and Juliet*, Shakespeare had written his play *King John* as a reaction against the anti-Catholic bias of an earlier play entitled *The Troublesome Reign of King John*. A few years later, Shakespeare wrote *Hamlet* in response to an earlier play that scholars now call the *Ur-Hamlet*, which was probably written by Thomas Kyd. Although Kyd's play has been lost to posterity, the fact that Kyd had been tried and imprisoned for atheism in 1593 suggests that Shakespeare had sought to "baptize" the story of Hamlet with his own profoundly Christian imagination. This revisiting of older works to correct their defects was employed once again in the writing of *King Lear*, in which Shakespeare clearly intends to counter the anti-Catholic bias of an earlier play, *The True Chronicle History of King Leir and His Three Daughters*, which was probably written by George Peele, and also in Shakespeare's writing of *Macbeth* to comment allusively upon an earlier play on a similar theme, *The Tragedy of Gowrie*, which had been banned, presumably by direct order of the king himself. Since this process of creative revisionism (to give it a name) seems part of Shakespeare's inspirational motivation in selecting a theme upon which to write, it would be a sin of critical

omission to fail to examine how Shakespeare's play con-
futes the bias of its source.

The bias of Arthur Brooke's *Tragicall Historye of Romeus
and Juliet* is scarcely difficult to detect. On the contrary, the
poem wears its author's anti-Catholicism on its sleeve, and
emblazons it across its proud and prejudiced chest:

> To this ende (good Reader) is this tragicall matter written,
> to describe unto thee a coople of unfortunate lovers, thrall-
> ing themselves to unhonest desire, neglecting the authoritie
> and advise of parents and frendes, conferring their principall
> counsels with dronken gossyppes, and superstitious friers
> (the naturally fitte instruments of unchastitie) attemptyng
> all adventures of peryll, for thattaynyng of their wished lust,
> using auriculer confession (the kay of whoredome, and
> treason) for furtheraunce of theyre purpose, abusing the
> honorable name of lawefull marriage, the cloke the shame
> of stolne contractes, finallye, by all means of unhonest lyfe,
> hastyng to most unhappy deathe.[2]

Having discussed the original source and motivation for
Shakespeare's writing of *Romeo and Juliet*, let's proceed to
a discussion of the play itself. Broadly speaking, it seems
that there are three ways of reading it. The first is the fatalistic reading in which fate and fortune are perceived as
omnipotent but blind and impersonal forces that crush the
"star-crossed lovers", and everyone else, with mechanical
indifference. In such a reading, free will, if it exists at all,
is utterly powerless to resist intractable Fate. If the fatalistic
reading is accepted, nobody is to blame for the events that
unfold throughout the play because there is nothing anyone can do to alter them.

[2] From the original Preface of Arthur Brooke's *Tragicall Historye of Romeus
and Juliet* (1562).

The second way of reading the play is what may be termed the feudal[3] or romantic reading, in which the feuding parties are held to blame for the tragic fate of the doom-struck and love-struck lovers. In such a reading, the hatred and bigotry of the Capulets and Montagues are the primary cause of all the woes, and the lovers are hapless victims of their parents' bloodlust who are nonetheless redeemed and purified by the passion and purity of their love for each other. In our day and age, this is perhaps the most widely accepted interpretation of the play's overarching morality or deepest meaning, harmonizing as it does with the ingrained romanticism and narcissism of the zeitgeist. Such a reading allows our contemporary epoch to moralize about "love" and "hate" without the imposition of conventional moral norms. It is the morality of John Lennon's "All You Need Is Love", a "love" that is rooted in the gratification of desire and has its antecedents in the Romanticism of Byronic self-indulgence.

The third way of reading the play is the cautionary or moral reading in which the freely chosen actions of each of the characters are seen to have far-ranging and far-reaching consequences. In such a reading, the animosity of the feuding parties and its consequences are weighed alongside the actions of the lovers, and those of other significant characters, such as Friar Laurence, Benvolio, Mercutio, the Prince, and the Nurse. Each is perceived and judged according to his actions and the consequences of those actions on others, and each is integrated into the whole picture so that the overriding and overarching moral may emerge. It is surely

---

[3] I am taking linguistic liberties, creating a neologism based etymologically upon the Old English *fæhthu* (enmity), from which "feud" is derived, as distinct from the common usage of "feudal", which has its roots in the Latin *feodum*, *feudum*, from which "feudal", "fee", and "fief" are derived, possibly from the original Frankish *fehod* (cattle property). See the *Concise Oxford Dictionary of Current English*, 5th ed. (Oxford: Oxford University Press, 1964).

significant, for instance, that *Romeo and Juliet* was written at around the same time as *The Merchant of Venice*, a play that is preoccupied with the whole question of freedom of choice and its consequences.[4] Clearly, such questions were at the forefront of the playwright's mind as he grappled with the hateful or besotted choices of his Veronese protagonists as they had been when he grappled with the choices facing his Venetian heroes and villains.

In spite of the blindness of many modern critics, it is clear from *Romeo and Juliet* itself, and from its place within the wider Shakespearean canon, that the only correct way of reading the play is the third way. It is, however, not the present writer who affirms this as an opinion but the play itself that insists upon it as a fact.

The play's opening scene shows us, in no uncertain terms, the ugliness of the world in which Romeo and Juliet are living. Sampson and Gregory, two servants of the house of Capulet, revel in the rivalry between the Capulets and their Montague enemies and indulge in salacious and uncouth reveries in which they fantasize about the rape of the Montague women. Thus, the vicious vindictiveness of the "ancient grudge" between the two noble households is exposed in the vile vernacular of their servants. The presence of such hatred is, however, merely the backdrop to the play's depiction of "love", or that which purports to be love but which is, in fact, a false and fallacious parody of it.

This false and fallacious love is first brought to our attention by Montague, Romeo's father, in his description

---

[4] *The Merchant of Venice* was probably written in late 1594 or, more likely, in 1595. As discussed already, the most likely date for the writing of *Romeo and Juliet* is 1595 or possibly 1596. For a full discussion of the role of choice and its consequences in *The Merchant of Venice*, see *Through Shakespeare's Eyes: Seeing the Catholic Presence in the Plays*, by Joseph Pearce (San Francisco: Ignatius Press, 2010), chaps. 6–7.

of his son's odd behavior, in which the play's prevailing metaphor of light-shunning darkness is introduced for the first time. Self-obsessed and obsessive "love" is an enemy of the light, making of itself "an artificial night" (1.1.138), locking itself into the introspective and private chambers of the self, and shutting up the windows of true perception. The consequences of such self-centered love are potentially self-destructive, a fact to which Shakespeare draws our attention in Montague's final ominous words:

> Black and portentous must this humor [mood] prove,
> Unless good counsel may the cause remove.
>
> (1.1.139–40)

This couplet not only contains the "black and portentous" prophecy of the play's tragic end but a crucial clue that "good counsel" is the necessary component in removing the causes of the portended tragedy. In the event, it is the almost total absence of "good counsel" that leaves Romeo and Juliet at the mercy of their own woeful passions.

Also embedded in these two lines is a significant clue that the feudal or romantic reading of the play is awry. If, as romantic readers of the play maintain, Romeo's love for Rosaline is false whereas his love for Juliet is true, there is nothing "black and portentous" about his "humor" because it will dissipate like the insubstantial thing that it is as soon as Romeo sets eyes on Juliet. Nor is "good counsel" necessary because Romeo's true love for Juliet will exorcise his false love for Rosaline without the need for counsel, good or bad. Montague's final lines are, therefore, worthless from the perspective of a feudal or romantic reading; and yet we must surely see these "black and portentous" words as potentially pregnant with meaning.

Since their deepest and most portentous meaning refers to the whole panoramic scope of the play, telescoping us from the opening scene of act 1 to a dark vision of the catastrophic and cataclysmic climax of the final scene of act 5, aren't we forced at least to consider the possibility that Shakespeare is being censorious about the nature of Romeo's love throughout the whole play, not only about its moping extravagance in the opening scenes? Such a conclusion is reinforced by the fact that the light-shunning metaphor, introduced in relation to Romeo's obsessive love for Rosaline, is maintained throughout the length of the play, especially in relation to Romeo's and Juliet's tragic love for each other.

Prior to any further discussion of this tragic love story, perhaps the most famous love story ever written, we should take a step back in order to look at love itself. What is love? And, equally important, what isn't love? Romeo, with the naïve certainty of youth, is confident that he has the answer:

> Love is a smoke rais'd with the fume of sighs;
> Being purg'd, a fire sparkling in lovers' eyes;
> Being vex'd, a sea nourish'd with loving tears.
> What is it else? A madness most discreet,
> A choking gall, and a preserving sweet.
>
> (1.1.188–92)

Love, for Romeo, is a blinding force; it is smoke that gets into the lover's eyes, a bitterness on which he chokes, and a vexatious sea in which he flounders. It is, to put the matter in a nutshell, mere "madness". It is, therefore, no surprise that Romeo confesses that, afflicted with such blindness and madness, he is utterly lost and does not know who he is:

I have lost myself; I am not here:
This is not Romeo, he's some other where.

(1.1.195–96)

In this adolescent discourse on the nature of love, Romeo will win no prizes for originality. To say that "love is blind" is, after all, one of the most hackneyed clichés that one can find. And this appears to be Shakespeare's point. Romeo's love for Rosaline is not the real thing. It is nothing but a shallow and trite cliché. What Romeo calls "love" isn't really love at all, at least it isn't love in the deeper and deepest sense of the word. Illustrating this, several critics have shown how Romeo's words parody the famous love sonnets of Petrarch, thereby reducing Romeo's declarations of love to the level of mere cliché.[5] This is made clear in Mercutio's mocking of Romeo's Petrarchan conceits:

Romeo! humours! madman! passion! lover!
Appear thou in the likeness of a sigh;
Speak but one rhyme and I am satisfied;
Cry but "Ay me!" pronounce but "love" and "dove".

(2.1.7–10)

Although Shakespeare uses the bawdy irreverence of Mercutio to make the connection between Romeo's unrequited love for Rosaline and Petrarch's unrequited love for Laura, we need to avoid the rash conclusion that Mercutio's voice is that of the playwright. On the contrary, his bawdy "realism" and contempt for Renaissance romance

---

[5] See, for instance, Crystal Downing, "A Rose by Any Other Name: The Plague of Language in *Romeo and Juliet*", and Rebecca Munro, "*Romeo and Juliet* and the Petrarchan Love Poetry Tradition", both published in the Ignatius Critical Edition of the play, pp. 165–81 and 229–44, respectively.

does not enable him to see or understand Romeo's "love" as coldly or clinically as he and his many critical admirers seem to believe. Mercutio, as a cynic, is even less capable of true love than is the lovesick Romeo, and, although he doesn't see it, he is even more blind to the reality of love than is the besotted young man he ridicules. He has no time for the numinous trappings of Petrarchan love and, believing that the numinous is merely nebulous, dismisses the "heavenly" as having its head in the clouds.

For Mercutio, the very antithesis of the Petrarchan lover, "love" is ultimately synonymous with fornication. He sees no distinction between love and lust, the former being a circumscribed and euphemistic expression of the latter, and the latter being merely the honest expression of the former. When Mercutio dies, we don't doubt that he has "known" women, in the euphemistic sense of the word, but we also know that he has never truly known women as true lovers know them, or as husbands know them. We have no trouble believing that Mercutio has lost his virginity, but we suspect that he has never lost his heart. As Romeo says, "He jests at scars that never felt a wound" (2.2.1), a riposte that, though unheard by Mercutio, is as telling in its insightful accuracy as anything Mercutio has uttered from his huge arsenal of punning wit. In speaking of love, Mercutio speaks of something of which he knows nothing. Whereas Romeo's wandering and wayward heart has lost sight of true love, Mercutio's hardened heart has locked love out. Romeo is looking for love in the wrong places; Mercutio refuses to look for it at all. Since, to succumb to a cliché, there are none so blind as those who will not see, Mercutio is more blind to the reality of love than the naïve and love-struck Romeo. It is not love that is blind but those who are blind to love.

Before we turn our attention to Juliet, the other "star-crossed lover" at the center of the tragedy, let's pause for a moment in the company of the elusive Rosaline. All that we know of her is learned from the mouths of others. She is the object of Romeo's lovelorn desire and the subject of Mercutio's scorn. But who is she? The most important clue is given by Romeo in his discussion about her with Benvolio in the play's opening scene, most specifically in his plaintive disdain for her vow of chastity:

> She'll not be hit
> With Cupid's arrow. She hath Dian's wit,
> And in strong proof of chastity well arm'd,
> From Love's weak childish bow she lives unharm'd.
> She will not stay the siege of loving terms,
> Nor bide th' encounter of assailing eyes,
> Nor ope her lap to saint-seducing gold.
>
> (1.1.206–12)

In these few pregnant lines, we learn enough about Rosaline to know that she is not elusively unattainable in the same sense as Petrarch's Laura. She is not simply, or at any rate she is not only, a poetic device. She is not a figment of idealized femininity, a personified abstraction of the ideal of *amour courtois*. She may remind us of Petrarch's Laura, or by a perverse leap of the imagination of Dante's Beatrice, and no doubt Shakespeare means her to remind us of these idols of courtly love, but she is much more than this. She is quite clearly a woman of flesh and blood who has been forced to repel Romeo's evidently clumsy and unwelcome advances. The imagery that Romeo employs is that of warfare, of his having put her under siege. She resists "the siege of loving terms" and avoids the "encounter of assailing eyes", reminding us more of Homer's Penelope than

Petrarch's Laura or Dante's Beatrice. And when the lover's full frontal assault had been repelled, she shuns the subtle charms of bribery or the promise of worldly fortune, refusing to open her lap to "saint-seducing gold". The sexual imagery is entirely appropriate considering that Romeo's intentions seem to be entirely sexual. He scorns her desire to remain chaste and treats with dismissive contempt her apparent claim that her vow of chastity is connected to her Christian convictions. She cannot "merit bliss" (1.1.220) by making him despair. She cannot merit heaven by sending him to hell. These words are worth contemplating carefully because they offer a key to Romeo's character and to his notions of "love". He is utterly self-absorbed, desiring to absorb his lover into his desire for self-gratification. Whereas true love is desiring the good of the other, Romeo desires that the other should feel good to him. He doesn't desire that his "love" go to heaven, he doesn't want her to "merit bliss", if it means being refused what he wants. In these lines, Romeo reveals himself as totally self-centered, the epitome of the impetuous adolescent. Indeed, if he weren't so young, we would have no hesitation in dubbing him a contemptible cad. This is worth remembering because it's only a matter of hours before he first sets eyes on Juliet. Does Juliet cause a miraculous change in the young man, teaching him how to love truly, as romantic readers of the play believe, or does his residual selfishness and self-absorption contribute to their downfall?

Juliet is introduced to us, significantly, immediately after the self-absorbed discourse by Romeo that we've just discussed. No sooner has Romeo finished waxing wistful about his failure to seduce Rosaline (at the close of act 1, scene 1) than we learn (in the opening lines of the following scene) of the woman who will take Rosaline's place as the object of his desire. It is also significant that, like

Rosaline, we are introduced to Juliet in her absence when
Capulet, her father, reminds Paris, her would-be suitor,
that she is still a child:

> My child is yet a stranger in the world.
> She hath not seen the change of fourteen years.
> Let two more summers wither in their pride
> Ere we may think her ripe to be a bride.
>
> (1.2.8–11)

When Paris responds that "younger than she are happy
mothers made" (1.2.12), Capulet's riposte is cutting: "And
too soon marr'd are those so early made" (1.2.13).

To put the matter bluntly and frankly, Shakespeare
makes it plain that Juliet is still a child, only thirteen years
old, barely a teenager. This singularly crucial fact is all too
often overlooked by modern critics who bestow upon her
an adulthood she does not possess.

The fact that Shakespeare is intent on stressing Juliet's
immaturity is apparent in his making Juliet two years
younger than her age in his source. In Brooke's *Tragicall
Historye of Romeus and Juliet*, she is almost sixteen, and in
another English version of the tragedy that Shakespeare
may have known, the translation of a novella by Matteo
Bandello, she is almost eighteen. It is also noteworthy
that in both these earlier versions the older Juliets were
still considered too young to marry. And yet Shakespeare
deliberately makes her even younger. His purpose for
doing so is clearly that he wants us to see Juliet as a child
who is thrown prematurely into an adult world in which
she not only loses her innocence but her life. This is the
heart of the tragedy.

Countering such a reading of the play, romantics will no
doubt stress that the youth of the lovers is merely a device

to highlight the unblemished purity of their true love. At the other extreme, cynical readers, taking their cue from Mercutio, will doubtless suggest that Shakespeare makes Juliet so young merely to show his male audience that Romeo is courting a true virgin. These two objections can be dismissed by closely scrutinizing the times in which Shakespeare was living and the moral and social conventions that prevailed in late Elizabethan England. Many social historians believe that children reached physical maturity, or puberty, later in sixteenth-century England than they do today. It is believed that girls matured at fourteen to fifteen, and boys at around sixteen.[6] As such, Juliet would have seemed even more of a child to Shakespeare's audience than she does to today's audiences. Youths under fifteen were still considered children, and early teenage marriages were rare indeed. Figures showing the age at first marriage during the period in which Shakespeare was writing indicate that only 6 percent of marriages were at the age of fifteen, and no figures are given for marriages below that age. Juliet was not yet fourteen when the action of the play takes place.[7] In the few cases on record in which children were married, they were not permitted to consummate their vows until much older.

Popular manuals of health in sixteenth-century England cautioned against the permanent damage to a young woman's health that could be caused by early marriage and its

---

[6] Lawrence Stone, *The Family, Sex and Marriage in England, 1500–1800* (New York: Harper, 1977), p. 512; Barbara Everett, *Young Hamlet: Essays on Shakespeare's Tragedies* (Oxford: Clarendon, 1989), p. 116; Ann Jennalie Cook, *Making a Match: Courtship in Shakespeare and His Society* (Princeton: Princeton University Press, 1991), pp. 17, 20; J. Karl Franson, " 'Too Soon Marr'd': Juliet's Age as Symbol in *Romeo and Juliet*", *Papers on Language and Literature* 32, no. 3 (1996): 244–62.

[7] Lawrence Stone, *The Crisis of the Aristocracy, 1558–1641* (Oxford: Clarendon, 1965), p. 654.

consummation, and by the childhood pregnancies that were its consequence. The grandmother of Anne Clopton, a contemporary of Shakespeare, opposed the proposed marriage of her thirteen-year-old granddaughter on the grounds of the "danger [that] might ensue to her very life from her extreme youth".[8] Such parental concern reflects Capulet's riposte to Paris that "too soon marr'd are those so early made", and it is surely significant that Shakespeare's own daughter Susanna was herself around Juliet's age when he was writing the play. As the father of a twelve-year-old daughter, Shakespeare's own perspective is that of a parent.

The general consensus in Elizabethan England was that marriage before sixteen was dangerous.[9] Elizabethan women married, on average, in their early to midtwenties, and men, on average, a few years later.[10] According to the historian Peter Laslett, who examined a thousand marriage licenses from the years immediately after Shakespeare wrote *Romeo and Juliet*, "the average age of ... Elizabethan and Jacobean brides was something like 24 and the average of bridegrooms was nearly 28."[11] The historian Christopher Hill noted that this is the oldest of any society known in history.[12] Shakespeare's own wife and his

[8] Ibid., p. 656.

[9] Ibid., pp. 656–57.

[10] Peter Laslett, *The World We Have Lost: English Society before the Coming of Industry* (New York: Scribner's, 1965), pp. 81–86; Stone, *Family, Sex and Marriage*, pp. 49, 490; Cook, *Making a Match*, pp. 265–67. The aristocracy married, on average, a little younger, due to arranged marriages designed to secure an heiress or to seal a political alliance, but even among the aristocracy the average spousal age at marriage at the time Shakespeare wrote *Romeo and Juliet* was twenty-one or twenty-two years of age.

[11] Laslett, *World We Have Lost*, p. 82.

[12] Christopher Hill, *The Collected Essays of Christopher Hill*, vol. 3, *People and Ideas in 17th Century England* (Brighton, England: Harvester, 1986), p. 195.

daughter Susanna conformed to the norms of Elizabethan society, marrying at about twenty-six and twenty-four, respectively, while his younger daughter, Judith, did not marry until she was thirty-one.

The literary critic J. Karl Franson concludes from this contextual evidence that Shakespeare's audience would have been shocked at Juliet's age and the way in which the child was propelled, unprepared, into an adult world with which she was ill-equipped to cope: "That Capulet would offer his daughter to Paris despite her 'extreme youth' ... must have been appalling to an Elizabethan."[13] Franson's overall conclusion is resoundingly and perceptively incisive. Juliet was "too soon marr'd" by the neglect or manipulation of callous and heartless adults. At the play's tragic heart is the broken heart of a child.

Romantic readers of the play are blind to such contextual evidence. Following their hearts and forsaking and forswearing their heads, they see the "love at first sight" between Romeo and Juliet as one of the most beautiful things in the whole drama. It is as pure and passionate as it is impetuous and impulsive. It is truly momentous, in the sense that it surrenders itself to the moment, and will not be assuaged by reason, temperance, or prudence. Such a love hurls itself heedlessly into the arms of the beloved, a headless heart hurtling toward a breathlessly exhilarating consummation. Shakespeare, who invariably and unerringly perceives the human condition with the incisive insight of genius, understands the exhilaration of this sort of love, and, from this moment onward, the whole action of the play accelerates. It is noteworthy, for instance, that Shakespeare condenses the whole drama into five breathless days, whereas in his source poem, the action takes place over several months. The question is not whether

[13] Franson, " 'Too Soon Marr'd' ".

Shakespeare understands such romantic passion; it is what he has to say about it.

In the first meeting between the two lovers, it is significant that Shakespeare selects sin as the prevailing metaphor for their first kiss. Unlike Rosaline, Juliet is clearly attracted by Romeo's charms and is torn between chaste decorum and erotic desire. As the mysterious stranger manipulates her words to serve his amorous purposes, bestowing the first kiss, the girl's struggle with her conscience is strained to the limit. This kiss, almost certainly Juliet's first, is a new and strange experience, throwing her into confusion. Her conflicted emotions are aroused still further by Romeo's indecorous use of a religious image: "Thus from my lips by thine my sin is purg'd" (1.5.105). The metaphor of the "sinful kiss" is taken literally by the naïve Juliet, causing her to exclaim in alarm that she has indeed shared in a sinful act in permitting herself to be kissed by the stranger: "Then have my lips the sin that they have took" (1.5.106). Her sense of sin is no doubt heightened by the erotic pleasure it had given her. Romeo, seizing the opportunity, manipulates her words once again to steal a second kiss: "Sin from my lips? O trespass sweetly urg'd! / Give me my sin again" (1.5.107–8).

Although romantic readers of this scene invariably bestow maturity on the thirteen-year-old, enabling her to play her part with a suave savoir faire belying her age, Shakespeare's use of the "sin" metaphor suggests a clear moral dimension to the exchange. The kiss does not merely transmit the sin metaphorically; it does so literally. The erotically charged Romeo has enflamed desire in the object of his advances, succeeding with Juliet where he had failed with the presumably more mature Rosaline.

The foregoing nonromantic reading of the lovers' first exchange seems to be vindicated by the words of the Chorus immediately after the scene we've just discussed:

Now old desire doth in his death-bed lie,
And young affection gapes to be his heir;
That fair for which love groan'd for and would die,
With tender Juliet match'd, is now not fair.
Now Romeo is belov'd, and loves again,
Alike bewitched by the charm of looks.

(2 Prol. 1–6)

The voice of the Chorus, being impartial and aloof, and therefore closest, presumably, to the narrative voice of the playwright, makes no distinction between the nature of Romeo's love for Rosaline and that which he has for Juliet. The "old desire" for Rosaline may be dead, but the "young affection" for Juliet desires eagerly to be "his heir". One "love" has simply been replaced by another in its likeness. Romeo is "belov'd, and loves again, / Alike bewitched by the charm of looks." Again, no distinction is made between the earlier love and its heir. Indeed, the Chorus seems to be suggesting that there *is* no distinction. Romeo simply "loves again". He has not spurned false love for true, but merely loves both women in the same way. In this sense, the phrase "alike bewitched" seems to have a double-meaning. Romeo and Juliet are "alike bewitched"—that is, bewitched by each other— but Romeo is also "alike bewitched" in that he was bewitched by Rosaline and Juliet alike. In both cases, he is bewitched by physical beauty, by "the charm of looks". And let's not forget that the love between Romeo and Juliet can be nothing but skin-deep and purely physical at this stage. Romeo and Juliet do not know each other. They do not even know each other's name. Romeo declares his "love" before he has even spoken a single word to his beloved. How can such love be anything but superficial, a bewitchment of the eye in response to great physical beauty? This, at any rate, seems to be the question that Shakespeare, via the Chorus, is asking.

The question is asked again, immediately, by Mercutio, in his savage lampooning of Petrarchan love (2.1.8–10)[14] and in his disdain for the "gossip Venus" and for Cupid, "her purblind son", the latter of whom he regards as a swindler and confidence trickster (2.1.11–12).[15] Mercutio sees Romeo as a victim of Venus, struck by Cupid's duplicitous dart, and as such, struck witless by love: "Romeo! humours! madman! passion! lover!" (2.1.7). For Mercutio, "Romeo", "madman", and "lover" are synonyms. Responding to Mercutio's jesting, the sober-minded Benvolio observes that Romeo is not so much a madman as a blind man who is at home in the darkness of his passions: "Blind is his love, and best befits the dark" (2.1.32).

And so, with Mercutio's description of Romeo's madness and Benvolio's lament at his blindness, and with the Chorus' suggestion that the young lover is still bewitched by the same enchantment that had overpowered him in the presence of Rosaline, we are prepared by Shakespeare for the breathless rush toward the tragic abyss, the self-destructive consequence of concupiscence. Throughout the remainder of the play, the palpable absence of the cardinal virtues of prudence and temperance paves the way for the denouement of the tragedy. The absence of such virtue in the lovers is exacerbated by its absence in other crucial characters who, being older, are perhaps even more culpable than the play's principal protagonists. Friar Laurence

---

[14] See the discussion about Shakespeare's satire on Petrarchan love on pages 37–38 above.

[15] Mercutio's description of Venus' partially blind son as "Young Abraham Cupid" (2.1.13) is an allusion to an "Abraham man", one of a class of beggars, thrown into poverty by the dissolution of the monasteries, who wandered the countryside feigning illness to obtain alms; i.e., Cupid is a beggarly conman.

begins by giving sagacious advice but fails to practice what he preaches in his rash agreement to marry the lovers in secret and with undue haste; Capulet begins with a seeming desire to protect his child from a premature marriage but then tries to force her to marry Paris; the Nurse fails to support Juliet, even suggesting that her young charge proceed with the bigamous marriage. It is clear, therefore, that Juliet is betrayed by those who should have saved her from her own immature folly. This failure on the part of the adult characters serves as a moral counterpoint to the treacherous passions of youth. It is as though Shakespeare is illustrating that the young will go tragically astray if not restrained by the wisdom, virtue, and example of their elders. The final tragedy is that this lesson is learned by the Capulets and Montagues only in the wake of the deaths of their children. The lesson *is* learned, however, and the consequent restoration of peace provides a sad but consoling catharsis. Whether such a cathartic turn can be considered a happy ending is a moot point. It is, however, an ending that restores not only peace but sanity and moral equilibrium to the surviving protagonists, and this is surely a source of joy, even if a joy tinted with sorrow.

Ultimately, the peace that reigns at the end of *Romeo and Juliet* is much greater than the worldly and merely political peace that emerges in Verona. It is the peace that surpasses all understanding, as St. Paul tells the Philippians (4:7), the peace that T. S. Eliot proclaims at the culmination and climax of *The Waste Land*, and the peace that descends on the so-called tragic climaxes of *Hamlet* and *King Lear*. Such peace is not of the sort that the world understands or desires. It is a peace that can be perceived only through the eyes of faith, a faith the world does not know and cannot offer, a faith that finds voice in the greatest art and finds the divine comedy in the midst of the greatest tragedies.

Chapter Three

Julius Caesar

Julius Caesar is one of the most popular of Shakespeare's plays and is on more high school curricula than any other of the Bard's works, with the possible exception of *Hamlet* and *Romeo and Juliet*. Such popularity, from a literary standpoint, is a little difficult to fathom. The play does not plumb the depths of the human condition in the manner of *Hamlet, Macbeth, Lear,* or *Othello,* nor does it soar to the heights of virtue in its depiction of heroes or heroines. Indeed, it could be argued, and has been argued, that the play lacks a hero of any sort. Its principal characters pale into relative insignificance and seem almost superficial in the company of the Prince of Denmark or the Thane of Cawdor. Shakespeare's Caesar, in the full pomp of his power, lacks the kingly majesty of Lear, which the latter retains even in the full degradation of his madness; Caesar's ghost is a pretty insubstantial waif beside the formidable presence of the ghost of Hamlet's father; Shakespeare's Brutus is a far less convincing idealist, even when adhering stoically to his ideals, than is Timon of Athens in his embittered disillusionment with his; and Shakespeare's Cassius is a pretty poor excuse for a cynically manipulative Machiavel when compared to Iago, King Claudius, or either of the diabolical Macbeths. Nor does

Julius Caesar boast a powerful feminine presence, which is such a vital force in many of Shakespeare's greatest plays. There is no *femme formidable* to imbue the drama with a feminine touch of sanity and sanctity. There is no Cordelia to prick the conscience of the king; no Isabella to tower over venality with moral rectitude; no Miranda to mirror the beauty and wonder of innocence; no Ophelia, whose very weakness exudes a powerful presence; no Desdemona, whose constancy marks her as a martyr. At the other end of the Bard's feminine spectrum, there are no *femmes fatales* whose very presence adds not only spice but poison to the Bard's simmering plots. There is no Didoesquely destructive Cleopatra; no demonically deadly Lady Macbeth; no treacherous Regan or Goneril. Instead, we are offered only two marginal and marginalized female characters, Calpurnia and Portia, whose presence is so sylph-like that we can almost forget that they are there. Calpurnia, Caesar's wife, is so insubstantial that she is cast aside by her husband with almost careless indifference. How different she is from the domineering Lady Macbeth, who brushes her husband's misgivings to one side with browbeating brusqueness. Similarly, Portia, Brutus' wife, is brushed aside by her husband, in spite of her entreaties. Her death offstage, lacking the potency or the pathos of Ophelia's offstage death, is almost shrugged off as a seeming irrelevance, or as a distraction from more important things. How different she is from Shakespeare's other Portia, the indomitable heroine of *The Merchant of Venice*, whose eloquence is perhaps unmatched anywhere else in Shakespeare's oeuvre.

Considering its relatively lightweight character, one wonders why *Julius Caesar* remains so enduringly popular. Leonard F. Dean, pondering this question in 1968, attributed it to extraliterary factors:

Because of its use in the schools, *Julius Caesar* is one of the best known of Shakespeare's plays, and yet it has not generally been talked about as a play. It probably got into the curriculum to begin with for institutional rather than dramatic reasons: the best possible English substitute for Latin, gives practice in public speaking, not sexy, easily cast in a boys' school, and so on. It apparently meant a great deal to nineteenth-century critics, but they thought of it not so much as a play as a collection of biographies, particularly of Brutus, an aristocrat whom they could praise and patronize at the same time.[1]

Dean's comments, written more than half a century ago, seem a trifle dated. Very few schools continue to teach Latin, removing the need to seek substitutes for it. The study of rhetoric is similarly no longer on high school curricula, so the play's rhetorically charged funeral orations are no longer valued for the practice they offer in public speaking. In a sexualized culture that has taken to reading *Romeo and Juliet* with the same breathless abandonment of reason that characterizes the play's "star-cross'd lovers", *Julius Caesar*'s not being "sexy" is no longer an attribute but a liability. The triumph of coeducation has threatened single-sex schools with extinction, so the fact that the almost complete absence of female characters made *Julius Caesar* "easily cast in a boys' school" is of negligible relevance in today's educational culture.

Pace Dean, *Julius Caesar* retains its popularity because it allows the designers of high school curricula to kill two birds with one stone. It serves not merely as literature but as history, enabling schools to teach Shakespeare and Roman history simultaneously. Like the nineteenth-century

---

[1] Leonard F. Dean, ed., *Twentieth Century Interpretations of Julius Caesar* (Englewood Cliffs, N.J.: Prentice-Hall, 1968), p. 1.

critics to whom Dean alludes, twenty-first-century teachers are often more concerned with *Julius Caesar*, "not so much as a play as a collection of biographies". To the extent that the life of Caesar and the circumstances surrounding his assassination continue to fascinate the imagination, it is scarcely surprising that a dramatic representation of one of the most famous chapters in human history by human history's most famous playwright is perennially popular.

Long before Shakespeare wrote his version, the story of Caesar's assassination had fascinated Elizabethan playgoers. As early as 1562, two years before Shakespeare's birth, the diarist Hanry Machyn referred to his seeing a dramatic performance of a play about Caesar. In 1594, as Shakespeare was establishing his own reputation as a playwright, the theatre owner Philip Henslowe recorded in his diary that his theatre company performed a two-part play about Caesar. Shakespeare must have been familiar with this play, and we can only conjecture the extent to which his own play, written some five years later, was a response to this earlier version.

All the evidence suggests that Shakespeare's *Caesar* was premiered some time in 1599. Thomas Platter, visiting London from Basle in Switzerland, noted that he had seen a play, *Vom ersten Keyser* (the first Caesar), on September 21, 1599, in a theatre on the south side of the Thames. Platter's dating of the play is confirmed by the writer John Weever, who refers to *Julius Caesar* in one of his own books, written in 1599.[2] Since Francis Meres does not include *Caesar* in the list of Shakespeare's plays in his *Palladis Tamia*,

---

[2] The reference appears in Weever's *The Mirror of Martyrs or the Life and Death of Sir John Oldcastle*. Although this was not published until 1601, Weever writes that it was "ready for the Press some two years ago"; i.e., it was written in 1599.

published in the autumn of 1598, it seems safe to date the play with some precision.

Other possible sources for Shakespeare's *Caesar* include Robert Garnier's *Cornélie*, translated into English by Thomas Kyd; the translation was published in 1594, five years before Shakespeare began work on his own play. In Garnier's five-act play, Caesar is very much the villain whose arrogance and wicked ambition brings about the destruction of all that is noble in the Roman Republic. Although Shakespeare must have known Kyd's translation, and although it is customary for critics to see parallels between Garnier's Caesar and Shakespeare's, it is perilous to see them too synonymously. Shakespeare's Caesar is certainly arrogant, but his ambition is treated somewhat ambivalently, so much so that it is almost eclipsed by the ambition of his enemies, particularly that of Cassius but, to a lesser extent, of Brutus also. Clearly, Shakespeare's perspective cannot be simplistically conflated with the anti-Caesarian tradition of sixteenth-century French drama. This being so, Shakespeare's begging to differ with the anti-Caesarian approach of Garnier and, by extension, with similar plays by earlier French writers, such as Marc-Antoine Muret and Jacques Grévin, suggests that he is uncomfortable with their enthusiasm for Caesar's assassins.

It would, of course, be a sin of omission to fail to mention Plutarch in a discussion of Shakespeare's sources for *Julius Caesar*. Plutarch's *Lives*, which contained biographical studies of Caesar, Brutus, and Antony, was written at the beginning of the second century. It would have been available to Shakespeare in Sir Thomas North's translation, published in 1579, and this is commonly assumed to have been the principal source for the play. Such a supposition, though perhaps justified, overlooks the fact that

Shakespeare was moving in dramatic circles and that in all probability he was moved primarily by what was unfolding on the Elizabethan stage. Thus, and as we have discussed already, his version of *Caesar* is probably indebted to the unknown play performed by Henslowe's company, to Kyd's translation of Garnier, and even, perhaps, to another anonymous play, *Caesar's Revenge*, which was not registered until 1606 but is believed to have antedated Shakespeare's play. Ultimately, Plutarch's seminal work deserves pride of place, not so much for its direct influence on Shakespeare, however pronounced and profound it might be, but for its role as the taproot from which all these various dramatizations stemmed. Nonetheless, it is likely that Shakespeare consulted North's translation of Plutarch in his preparation for writing the play, and it is clear that his overarching moral perspective mirrors that of Plutarch. Shakespeare, like Plutarch, represents the people of Rome as fickle and confused and as being easily manipulated by the skillful use—or abuse—of rhetoric. Like Plutarch, Shakespeare depicts Cassius as someone motivated more by personal hatred of Caesar than by any political principles. Also following Plutarch, Shakespeare paints Brutus somewhat sympathetically but as being culpable for his actions, particularly in his allowing himself to be duped by Cassius and in his imprudent and intemperate hastiness in joining the conspiracy. Echoing Plutarch's political reading of events, Shakespeare illustrates that the conspiracy not only fails in its objective to bring liberty and order to Rome but is the harbinger of anarchy, from which a succession of tyrants would emerge. Shakespeare, like Plutarch, is more concerned with moral character than with historical fact, concentrating on the consequences of the good or bad motives and choices of the human person. As with Plutarch, Shakespeare uses history to teach perennial lessons about the nature of man.

When we approach Shakespeare's Caesar, the play's eponymous character and its alleged "hero", we are shocked by the discrepancy between the enormous presence of the public persona and the pathetic reality of the private man. On the one hand, Caesar is the most powerful man in the Western world; on the other, he is prone to physical maladies and is seen to be both physically and morally weak. This anomalous abyss separating the image from the reality is present in the very form of the play. While Caesar is the eponymous hero of the whole drama, the star of the show, whose name appears in lights as the one who lends his name to the play's title, he is only a peripheral character, brushed aside by Brutus as contemptuously as Caesar brushes aside the protestations of his wife. Compared to Brutus and Cassius, he has a minor role, even in his own play, and it is ironic that his power resides not in the vacuous nature of his words but in the vacuum created by his absence. Caesar's lines in the play are among the least memorable, especially when compared to the funeral orations of Brutus or Antony, or the Machiavellian asides of Cassius. Furthermore, his relatively few lines serve to highlight his lack of judgment and his hypocrisy. Almost the first thing he does is ignore the warnings of the Soothsayer that he should "beware the ides of March" (1.2.18, 23).[3] Dismissing the true prophet of his own impending doom as "a dreamer", he exits immediately afterward, with all his entourage, leaving only Brutus and Cassius on stage. Thus, within moments of Caesar's impetuous dismissal of the words of the prophet, we see Cassius poisoning the ear of Brutus, thereby laying the foundations for the assassination that the Soothsayer had prophesied.

When we next see Caesar, he is expressing his distrust of Cassius to Antony:

---

[3] *Julius Caesar*, ed. Joseph Pearce, Ignatius Critical Editions (San Francisco: Ignatius Press, 2012). Text references are to act, scene, and line.

Caesar. Let me have men about me that are fat;
Sleek-headed men, and such as sleep o' nights.
Yond Cassius has a lean and hungry look;
He thinks too much. Such men are dangerous.

Antony. Fear him not, Caesar, he's not dangerous;
He is a noble Roman, and well given.

Caesar. Would he were fatter! But I fear him not.
Yet if my name were liable to fear,
I do not know the man I should avoid
So soon as that spare Cassius. He reads much,
He is a great observer, and he looks
Quite through the deeds of men. He loves no plays,
As thou dost, Antony; he hears no music.
Seldom he smiles, and smiles in such a sort
As if he mock'd himself, and scorn'd his spirit
That could be mov'd to smile at anything.
Such men as he be never at heart's ease
Whiles they behold a greater than themselves,
And therefore are they very dangerous.
I rather tell thee what is to be fear'd
Than what I fear; for always I am Caesar.
Come on my right hand, for this ear is deaf,
And tell me truly what thou think'st of him.

(1.2.192–214)

Here we see Caesar at his most prescient but also at his most preposterous. We know that he is right to mistrust Cassius because we have just witnessed Cassius in the seditious act of tempting Brutus. Yet he refuses to act upon his private fears because his artificially constructed public persona must appear to be fearless. Caesar, the self-deified ruler of the known world, does not know fear. As with his dismissal of the Soothsayer, his dismissal of his justifiable fears about Cassius show that Caesar's idolization of himself, his deification of the figment of himself that he has created, cushions him from any sensibility of the real mortal danger that he is facing.

Embedded within this speech is a metadramatic reference to the turbulent politics of Shakespeare's own day. Caesar's reference to Cassius as one who is not to be trusted because "he loves no plays" and "hears no music" is clearly an attack on the Puritans in Elizabethan England, who considered the theatre and dancing to be sinful and who were against the use of polyphony or chant in the liturgy. Caesar's words are a reiteration of the words of Lorenzo in the final act of *The Merchant of Venice*, which Shakespeare had written three or four years earlier:

> The man that hath no music in himself,
> Nor is not moved with concord of sweet sounds,
> Is fit for treasons, stratagems, and spoils;
> The motions of his spirit are dull as night,
> And his affections dark as [Erebus]:
> Let no such man be trusted. Mark the music.
>
> (5.1.83–88)[4]

As is so often the case in Shakespeare's plays, the villain is tagged by these topical references as both a Machiavellian and a Puritan, reminding us that Shakespeare was always writing with his own turbulent time in mind, even when his theme is ostensibly connected to the distant past or to distant countries. We should remind ourselves that political and religious censorship prevailed in Elizabethan England so that it was impossible for a playwright to write openly about political and religious issues. In choosing to set his plays in the past or in foreign countries, such as Italy, he could give his plays a convivial Catholic setting without incurring the

---

[4] *The Merchant of Venice*, ed. Joseph Pearce, Ignatius Critical Editions (San Francisco: Ignatius Press, 2009).

wrath of the censors. Even then, an element of circumspection and due decorum was essential. At the very time that Shakespeare was writing *Julius Caesar*, the Anglican church, in what became known as the Bishops' Ban, was seeking to suppress dissident and dissenting voices on the stage. On June 1, 1599, the Archbishop of Canterbury, John Whitgift, and the Bishop of London, Richard Bancroft, issued a ban on certain works and ordered that no further English history plays be printed unless approved by the Queen's Privy Council—that is, the government. It is notable, for instance, that Shakespeare wrote no further English history plays after this ban was imposed, suggesting that his own work was considered suspect by the authorities.[5] Thereafter, he often chose ancient Rome as the historical settings for his plays, circumventing the ban. This may also have been the reason that Shakespeare chose to write on Caesar at this particular time and not earlier.

The next time we see Caesar is in act 2, when his wife, Calphurnia, is endeavoring to dissuade him from going to the Senate. She had been beset with nightmares during the previous night, in which she had seen visions of her husband being murdered. She is further troubled by reports of "horrid sights" (2.2.16) throughout the city during the previous night's storm, corroborating the stories recounted by Casca and Cinna at the end of act 1. As with the horrors of the storm in *Macbeth*, Shakespeare evokes the way that natural and supernatural forces roar in outrage at the foul deeds of sinful men, and, as with the vision of the Ghost at the beginning of *Hamlet*, he is at pains to cite several independent witnesses to establish the objectivity

[5] Although *Henry VIII* is believed to be by Shakespeare, at least in part, it does not seem to have been written until 1612 or 1613, after Shakespeare had retired to Stratford, many years after the ban, and several years after Whitgift's and Bancroft's deaths.

and authenticity of the visions, precluding the possibility
of explaining the portents away as mere hallucinations.
Once again, as with the case of the Soothsayer, Caesar has
been given ample warning of the mortal danger in which
he finds himself, and once again he dismisses the warnings.
When the augurs, having made sacrifice to the gods, con-
firm Calphurnia's fears, adding their voice to hers in advis-
ing Caesar not to venture forth from his home because
of the portents of doom they have received, he remains
dismissively aloof:

> Caesar should be a beast without a heart,
> If he should stay at home to-day for fear.
> No, Caesar shall not. Danger knows full well
> That Caesar is more dangerous than he:
> We are two lions litter'd in one day,
> And I the elder and more terrible;
> And Caesar shall go forth.
>
> (2.2.42–48)

Although Caesar's defiance of death exhibits the outward markings of commendable courage, he is betrayed
by his false vision of himself. Caesar does not need to
fear danger because Caesar is more dangerous than fear
itself. He is older and more terrible than fear. This self-
deification is not merely pompous but is also pathetic. As
we watch Caesar put himself upon an Olympian pedes-
tal, we don't know whether to laugh or cry. Indeed, the
whole scene descends from pathos to bathos when Caesar
is ultimately duped into believing that all the omens were
good portents by the deliberate deception of one of the
conspirators, Decius Brutus, who had earlier boasted that
he could manipulate Caesar to do his will through the
use of flattery. The irony is that the mighty Caesar, who
likens himself to a god, is in fact nothing more than one

of the "gilded butterflies" that the wizened Lear laughs at in his hard-earned wisdom. Caesar, for all his supercilious grandiloquence, flutters to his death on the wings of flattery.

En route to the Capitol, Caesar is met once again by the persistent Soothsayer, who repeats his warning, and also by Artemidorus, a teacher of rhetoric, who endeavors to give Caesar a note warning him of the conspiracy. Both men are dismissed with blithe indifference as Caesar proceeds with impregnable ignorance to his doom. His final moments are pregnant with irony as he boasts that he will not succumb to flattery, which he describes as the "sweet words, / Low-crooked curtsies, and base spaniel fawning" (3.1.42–43) "that which melteth fools" (3.1.42). Considering that he has just been fooled by flattery, a flattery that will fell him fatally, he is, by his own definition, a fool whose life is about to melt away in the heat of its own folly. His last speech is full of pomposity and arrogance, culminating in one final bombastic act of hubris, in which he likens his immutable will to that of "Olympus", before he is cut down (3.1.74). The final irony and the final Shakespearean insult to Caesar's majesty reside in the fact that his final words, his most famous, point not to his own majesty but to the triumph of his nemesis: "Et tu, Brute?—Then fall, Caesar!" (3.1.77). As Caesar falls from his self-constructed and misconstructed Olympus, the enormity of his fall is dwarfed by the enormity of Brutus' treachery.

Although Shakespeare's Caesar is a somewhat pathetic figure, it is a grievous misreading of the play to see his assassination as justifiable or even praiseworthy. Cassius, the progenitor of the plot to kill Caesar, is clearly the play's overarching villain. Motivated by hatred and envy, and prone to corruption, Cassius is cast in the role of the

Machiavel, the cynical manipulator who appears in many
of Shakespeare's plays. He is numbered with Iago, King
Claudius, Polonius, Edmund, Richard III, and the Macbeths as those without faith or principle who prey upon the
virtuous and godly. It is inconceivable that a plot hatched
by such a serpent could be seen as justifiable. The villainy
of Brutus is by no means as obvious but is nonetheless as
real. His high ideals do not excuse his low actions, and he
reminds modern readers perhaps of the many deadly ideal-
ists who have washed themselves clean, as they see it, in the
blood of their victims. We think perhaps of Robespierre
and the Reign of Terror, Lenin and the Gulag Archipelago, or Hitler and the Holocaust. It is also interesting that
Brutus is condemned unequivocally as a villain in the only
critical judgment of Brutus' character from Shakespeare's
own time. The poet John Weever, writing in the very year
that *Julius Caesar* was first staged, passes this poetic judgment on the viciousness of Brutus:

> The many-headed multitude were drawne
> By Brutus speach, that Caesar was ambitious,
> When eloquent Mark Antonie had showne
> His vertues, who but Brutus then was vicious?[6]

The most convincing argument against the casting of
Brutus as a villain is the final laudatory judgment of him by
Antony in the play's final scene:

> This was the noblest Roman of them all.
> All the conspirators save only he

[6] Weever, *Mirror of Martyrs or Life and Death of Sir John Oldcastle*, quoted in
Oscar James Campbell and Edward G. Quinn, eds., *The Reader's Encyclopedia of
Shakespeare* (New York: MJF Books, 1966), p. 411.

Did that they did in envy of great Caesar;
He only in a general honest thought
And common good to all made one of them.
His life was gentle; and the elements
So mix'd in him that Nature might stand up
And say to all the world, "This was a man!"
                              (5.5.68–75)

There is no doubt that eulogistic lines in this vein are normally reserved at the culmination of Shakespeare's plays
for those who are truly worthy of them. Indeed, it could
be that the melting and mellowing of Brutus' stoically
hardened heart in the play's final scenes constitutes a genuine conversion to a Christian concept of charity.[7] Perhaps
so. On the other hand, the rhetorical device that Shakespeare employs throughout the play is that of irony. Is it
not ironic that these words are spoken by the rhetorically
manipulative Antony, whose nobility dissolves with his
first bloodlustful taste of real power? Do we believe him?
Are we meant to believe him?

In the final analysis, the most striking feature of *Julius
Caesar* is that none of its principal characters are particularly
virtuous. This is not unique in the Shakespearean canon.
We think perhaps of *Romeo and Juliet*, in which none of
the characters show much virtue except for the fatally
flawed Friar. It is, however, unusual to see the absence of
virtue to such a striking degree. It is not like the Shakespeare that we know and love. And herein lies another
solution to the problem we posed earlier with regard to
the secret of the play's popularity in the modern academy.
The postmodern academy is uncomfortable with morality;

---

[7] See Sophia Mason, "Brutus in Hell", essay published in the Ignatius Critical Edition of the play, pp. 173–79.

it has squeezed virtue from the curriculum with its vice-like grip; it has an unhealthy disdain for the healthy. It thrives on moral ambiguity and ambivalence. It is no wonder that it is at home with the apparent moral ambivalence of the characters in *Julius Caesar*. It is also no wonder that it is at home with the high degree of irony with which Shakespeare spices his plot. The sneer of irony is the cynical grin on the face of most postmodern criticism. It is the only humor with which it is entirely comfortable. It is, therefore, not surprising that the academy is comfortable with *Julius Caesar*, a play that is full of endearing sinners and is not polluted by the grace of sanctity.

And yet are we really meant to believe that the same playwright who wrote so many other plays that are permeated throughout with Christian realism and orthodox Christian theology also wrote a work of nihilistic irony? Evidently, if we are reading the play as the postmoderns are reading it, we can't be reading it as it was written or as it was meant to be performed or read. How then should we read it?

As with all literature, it should be read through the eyes of the author, as far as this is possible, which in Shakespeare's case means reading it through the eyes of an orthodox Christian living in Elizabethan England. When we read the play through these eyes, which are so much more lucid than our own or those of today's hopelessly wayward critics, we see the same profound morality emerging that we see in his other works. On the most obvious level, Shakespeare is echoing the words of Mercutio in *Romeo and Juliet*. He is calling down a plague on all their houses, in the sense that he is pouring scorn on Caesar's vanity, on Antony's bloodthirsty opportunism, on Cassius' ambition, on Brutus' brutal idealism. Yet, unlike Mercutio, he is cursing not from the perspective of a worldly cynicism but from that of a believing Christian at a time when believing Christians were being tortured and put to death by the vanity of monarchs, by bloodthirsty opportunists, by political ambition, and by brutal idealism.

There is, however, a deeper level of meaning that is all too often overlooked completely. It is the sound of silence within the play, the scream in the vacuum of the play's vacuity, the unheard and unheeded voice of the virtuous. It is the voice of Calphurnia, which, if heeded, would have saved Caesar's life; it is the voice of Portia, which, if heeded, might have urged Brutus to think twice about his involvement with the conspirators. It is the voice of the Soothsayer and of the augurs. It is the voice of Artemidorus, a teacher of rhetoric, whose note to Caesar is devoid of all rhetorical devices and direct to the point of bluntness:

> Caesar, beware of Brutus; take heed of Cassius; come not near Casca; have an eye to Cinna; trust not Trebonius; mark well Metellus Cimber; Decius Brutus loves thee not; thou hast wrong'd Caius Ligarius. There is but one mind in all these men, and it is bent against Caesar. If thou beest not immortal, look about you. Security gives way to conspiracy. The mighty gods defend thee! (2.3.1–6)

The note is not read, the voice is not heard, and the consequences are fatal.

All that was missing in the play is the one thing necessary: the still, small voice of calm that the proud refuse to hear.

Chapter Four

Othello

One of the four great tragedies—alongside *Hamlet, King Lear*, and *Macbeth*—*Othello* is among the darkest of Shakespeare's plays, illumining the shadows of the gloomiest recesses of the human psyche and serving as a damning indictment of the world in which it was written.

A survey of the situation in England at the time of the play's composition will enable the modern reader to understand something of Shakespeare's motives for writing such a gloom-laden and doom-laden tragedy. First performed on All Saints' Day (November 1) 1604, *Othello* was written in the second year of the reign of James I, who had acceded to the throne in March 1603.

James was the only son of Mary Stuart, Queen of Scots, who had been executed on the orders of James' predecessor, Elizabeth I, in 1587. Mary was considered by Catholics to be a martyr for the Catholic faith, a view that was expressed with beauty and eloquence by the Jesuit poet Robert Southwell, whom Shakespeare probably knew and to whose poetry Shakespeare alludes in several of his plays. Southwell's poem "Decease Release", written in the first person with the Queen of Scots as the narrator, casts the queen as "pounded spice", the fragrance of which ascends to heaven:

God's spice I was and pounding was my due,
In fading breath my incense savored best,
Death was the mean my kernel to renew,
By lopping shot I up to heavenly rest.[1]

Although the poem is clearly Southwell's tribute to the executed Queen of Scots, its being written in the first person gave it added potency following Southwell's own execution in 1595. Like the martyred queen of whom he wrote, Southwell was also "pounded spice" whose essence is more pleasing and valued for being crushed: "God's spice I was and pounding was my due." Shakespeare was clearly alluding to this line of Southwell's poem in *King Lear*, written a year or so after *Othello*, in Lear's use of the phrase "God's spies" (5.3.17), a play on "God's spice" but also a veiled reference to Jesuits, such as Southwell, who were "traitors" in the eyes of the Elizabethan and Jacobean state but were "God's spies" and "God's spice" in the eyes of England's Catholics. As a Jesuit in Elizabethan England, Southwell had been one of "God's spies" who, being caught, became "God's spice", ground to death that he might receive his martyr's reward in heaven. "Upon such sacrifices," Shakespeare exclaims through the lips of Lear, "the gods themselves throw incense" (5.3.21).[2]

Unlike his mother, James was not a Catholic, having been raised as a Protestant, but he had hinted heavily that he would introduce religious toleration should he become king. At first it appeared that the new king was as good as his word. In the first year of his reign, it was decreed that

[1] James H. McDonald and Nancy Pollard Brown, *The Poems of Robert Southwell, S.J.* (London: Oxford University Press, 1967), pp. 47–48. The spelling has been modernized for purposes of clarification.

[2] *King Lear*, ed. Joseph Pearce, Ignatius Critical Editions (San Francisco: Ignatius Press, 2008). Text references are to act, scene, and line.

fines and other penalties would no longer be imposed for recusancy, the "crime" of refusing to attend Anglican services on grounds of religious conscience. With the onerous pecuniary burden removed, thousands of conforming or closet Catholics stayed away from Anglican services and sought once again to practice their faith fully and openly. "It was at once apparent," wrote Heinrich Mutschmann and Karl Wentersdorf, "that Elizabeth's policy of extermination had not achieved its purpose, and that Catholicism still constituted a formidable power in most parts of the country."[3]

Fearing a resurgent and resurrected Catholicism, Parliament immediately began to put pressure on the king to reintroduce penal measures against the "papists". In February 1604, James yielded to the intense pressure and once more banished all Catholic priests from the country. In July 1604, a bill was passed that confirmed all the Elizabethan statutes against recusants. Armed with this new draconian law against religious freedom, the authorities renewed their persecution of Catholics with vigor. The short-lived joy of the Catholics was plunged into the abyss of despair, their hopes dashed by the knowledge that James had reneged on all his promises of religious toleration. This sense of desolation or despondency was summarized by the Shakespeare scholar and historian Hildegard Hammerschmidt-Hummel:

In the 1590's ... many of Elizabeth I's subjects ... looked to the Scottish king with hope and expectation, thinking that James would relieve their plight. They were soon disappointed. The king's proclamations that the anti-Catholic

---

[3] H. Mutschmann and K. Wentersdorf, *Shakespeare and Catholicism* (New York, Sheed & Ward, 1952), pp. 27–28.

penal laws would remain unchanged were in stark contrast to his earlier statements. The secret Catholics in England, the Catholics-in-exile and even the powers in Rome, accused James of breaking his word and of treachery. There was much anger, particularly among the sons of the Catholic gentry in the Midlands who had suffered particularly badly under the anti-Catholic legislation and had sustained great financial losses.... The Catholics must have regarded James I as a fallen angel, as Lucifer himself. Within a very short period, their plight became even worse than it had been under Elizabeth I.[4]

Many Catholics had held on to their faith grimly, in the knowledge that the aging queen could not live forever and in the hope that things would be better under James. Now they were faced with the dark and stark reality that there would be no respite under the new king. For some, this was the final straw. Realizing that there was no immediate prospect of religious liberty, many succumbed at last to the state religion, conforming reluctantly; others were tempted to violence as a last desperate effort to restore the faith of their fathers. Whereas the former group had surrendered, the latter group became involved in various plots to kill or kidnap the king and his ministers, culminating in the following year with the notorious Gunpowder Plot.

As a Catholic himself, Shakespeare would have shared with his co-religionists an intense anger toward the king and would have experienced the deep sense of desolation at the renewal of the persecution, following as it did so soon after the initial exhilaration at the queen's death and the king's accession. Shakespeare's own father had been fined for his Catholicism in 1592, and his daughter would

---

[4] Hildegard Hammerschmidt-Hummel, *The Life and Times of William Shakespeare 1564–1616* (London: Chaucer Press, 2007), p. 261.

be fined for her Catholic faith in 1606. It is, therefore, no surprise that the plays written after the renewal of the persecution, *Othello*, *King Lear*, and *Macbeth*, are among Shakespeare's darkest. It is the apparent morbidity of plays such as these that led G. K. Chesterton to describe Shakespeare as being "delirious".[5] In truth, the plays were no more delirious than the times in which the playwright lived, times in which an Edmund or Iago lurked with Machiavellian menace in the corridors of power, and times where faith itself was not only feverish but oftentimes deadly. They were times that were encapsulated in the closing lines of *King Lear*, Shakespeare's most delirious play:

> The weight of this sad time we must obey,
> Speak what we feel, not what we ought to say.
> The oldest hath borne most: we that are young
> Shall never see so much, nor live so long.
>
> (5.3.325–28)

Considering the darkness of the times and the treachery of the king in reneging on his promise of religious tolerance, it is likely that Shakespeare makes an allusive connection between King James and the character of Iago, the Machiavellian monster at the dark and deadly heart of *Othello*. In the source from which he drew inspiration for the play, Cinthio's *Hecatommithi*, Shakespeare changed the name of Alfiero, the Machiavellian character, to Iago, a Spanish variant of the name "James", thereby deliberately connecting his ruthless and cynical villain with England's new king. He also changed the villain's motive from that of an adulterous lust in the original source to that of a deep-rooted political and philosophical cynicism, mirroring the

---

[5] G. K. Chesterton, *Chaucer* (London: Faber & Faber, 1932), p. 12.

sordid reality of Jacobean *realpolitik*, in his own version of the story.

At this juncture, it is worth noting that all four of Shakespeare's great tragedies are characterized by the potent presence of the irreligious and morally iconoclastic Machiavel. In *Hamlet*, King Claudius poisons Denmark with his ruthless and murderous deception, assisted somewhat ineptly by his spymaster Polonius; in *King Lear*, a menagerie of Machiavels (Edmund, Regan, Goneril, and Cornwall) brutalize Britain and ultimately each other in self-destructive self-assertion; in *Macbeth*, the murderous and treacherous Macbeths form a double-entente, dabbling with diabolism on the road to ruin. And yet it could be argued that Iago upstages all of his unwholesome rivals as the Master Machiavel, at least in terms of his sheer nastiness and lack of redeeming qualities. King Claudius has moments of near repentance that humanize him, teasing a degree of reluctant sympathy from the audience; Edmund's illegitimacy paradoxically legitimizes, up to a point, the resentment that animates his actions; even the Macbeths have vestiges of virtue, as seen in Macbeth's noble and courageous beginning, all too soon perverted, or Lady Macbeth's niggling conscience, manifested in her final madness. Iago, on the other hand, seems to be malice personified, a manifestation of manifold vice with no discernible vestiges of grace. This is the reason that many critics have seen him as little more than a personified abstraction, signifying vice or malignity itself. Many have seen parallels with the figure of the Vice in medieval morality plays, in which the human personality of the character is sacrificed in order to demonize the vice itself. If this is so, as seems pretty incontrovertible, it transforms Iago into a trope or type, crudely allegorical, in which he is deprived of personhood and personality, the traits of a fully human character, in order to accentuate the moral to which he points. Iago is dehumanized so that he can be demonized. He is monstrous so that he might be a monstrance, showing forth the moral that the playwright wishes to demonstrate to his audience. Once this is understood, the full power of Shakespeare's choice of Iago— that is, James—as the name for his monstrous Machiavel becomes startlingly apparent.

In the very first scene of the play, Iago reveals himself in starkly satanic terms with his declaration that "I am not what I am" (1.1.66), the antithesis of God's declaration of Himself in Scripture as "I AM THAT I AM."[6] A couple of scenes later, Iago responds scornfully to Roderigo, dismissing the very notion of virtue and the grace that is necessary for its practice: "Virtue? A fig! 'Tis in ourselves that we are thus and thus" (1.3.319). In this solitary line, Iago declares himself to be not only a non-Christian but an anti-Christian. He is *homo superbus* (prideful man) who believes that he has the power to be what he wants to be without the need for God. Having hatched the plot to bring about Othello's downfall, his proclamation of his intention to bring it to destructive fruition is expressed in unequivocally demonic terms: "I ha't. It is engender'd. Hell and night / Must bring this monstrous birth to the world's light" (1.3.397–98). Later, as the plot thickens and darkens, Iago is even more brazen in his devil worship and the cynical deception it demands:

> Divinity of hell!
> When devils will their blackest sins put on,
> They do suggest at first with heavenly shows,
> As I do now.
>
> (2.3.339–42)

[6] *Othello*, ed. Joseph Pearce, Ignatius Critical Editions (San Francisco: Ignatius Press, 2014). Exodus 3:14 (Geneva Bible, 1599).

Iago's deceitful words "pour [a] pestilence into [Othello's] ear" (2.3.345), enflaming the Moor's latent jealousy through the insinuation that Desdemona is in an adulterous relationship with Cassio, thereby poisoning the Moor's love for his hapless wife.

Iago's pouring of the pestilence into Othello's ear reminds us of Claudius' pouring of poison into the ear of Hamlet's father, a murderous act that is itself a metaphor for the lies poured into the ears of those whom Claudius deceives for his own cynical ends. As *Hamlet* and *Othello* both testify, envenomed words are as poisonous and as deadly as envenomed swords, a grim fact of which the venomous Iago is only too aware:

> The Moor already changes with my poison:
> Dangerous conceits are in their natures poisons,
> Which at the first are scarce found to distaste,
> But, with a little act upon the blood,
> Burn like the mines of sulphur.
>
> (3.3.329–33)

Here, however, it is not Iago's words alone that are poisonous but the "dangerous conceits" in Othello's prideful heart. It is the Moor's violent jealousy, itself the bitter fruit of his pride, that is venomous. Iago will simply use the canker of jealousy already eating away at Othello's heart to manipulate the Moor's own downfall. Iago is the tempter, the disseminator of lies and half-truths, but it is the poison inherent in Othello's own sinful nature, his "dangerous conceits", that will cause his blood to burn like the sulfurous pits of hell. Thus, Iago's role is that of Satan and Othello's that of sinful Adam, man himself, who falls through the folly of his own pride. It is the Moor's own tragic flaw, his prideful jealousy, that leads to the forsaking of his love for Desdemona, and it is his demonic invocation of the power of hell itself that turns his love into hate:

> Look here, Iago—
> All my fond love thus do I blow to heaven.
> 'Tis gone.
> Arise, black vengeance, from the hollow hell!
> Yield up, O love, thy crown and hearted throne
> To tyrannous hate! Swell, bosom, with thy fraught,
> For 'tis of aspics' tongues!
>
> (3.3.448–54)

In exorcising the love for Desdemona from his heart, dispatching it contemptuously to the heaven he has also rejected, he exorcises heaven itself and its grace, yielding his heart to a tyrant (jealousy) that fills it with the serpent's venom. It is, therefore, necessary to refute the misreading of the play by many critics, of whom A.C. Bradley is the most prominent, who see Othello as a noble and largely blameless figure who is merely a victim of Iago's treachery.[7] Other critics, such as F.R. Leavis, have argued convincingly that it is Othello's tragic flaw, his prideful jealousy, that makes the play an authentic tragedy.[8] It is Othello's jealousy that blinds him to the truth of his wife's innocence, and it is this same prideful blindness that makes him such a credulous dupe of Iago's malevolent plans. *Othello* can be considered a true tragedy precisely because the hero is culpable for his own catastrophic fall.

If, however, Othello is not the noble figure painted by Bradley, does Shakespeare's negative depiction of him indicate a degree of racism on Shakespeare's part? Although

---

[7] See A.C. Bradley, *Shakespearean Tragedy* (London: Macmillan, 1904).
[8] See F.R. Leavis, *The Common Pursuit* (London: Chatto & Windus, 1952).

this has been argued by some critics, such arguments are ultimately untenable.

The lines most often quoted to justify claims of racism on Shakespeare's part are those from the play's opening scene in which Iago informs Brabantio, Desdemona's father, that Othello is fornicating with his daughter:

> Even now, now, very now, an old black ram
> Is tupping your white ewe. Arise, arise;
> . . . .
> Or else the devil will make a grandsire of you.
> Arise, I say.
>
> (1.1.89–90, 92–93)

These are indeed offensive words, but let's not forget that they are being uttered by an offensive person. Iago may indeed be a racist, but since he is also a thinly disguised depiction of the devil himself, it can hardly be argued from the words that Shakespeare places in Iago's demonic mouth that Shakespeare is himself a racist. On the contrary, since we are clearly meant to dislike Iago and everything for which he stands, might it not be more convincingly argued that Shakespeare means his audience to find Iago's racist language distasteful? To argue that Shakespeare is a racist because of the words of Iago is akin to arguing that he is a relativist because of Polonius' words in *Hamlet* to his son Laertes that there is no higher truth than being true to oneself ("This above all: To thine own self be true" [1.3.78][9]), or that Shakespeare is a nihilist because of Macbeth's final judgment on what he perceives to be the meaninglessness of life ("Life's ... a tale / Told by an idiot, full of sound and fury, / Signifying nothing" [5.5.24,

---

[9] *Hamlet*, ed. Joseph Pearce, Ignatius Critical Editions (San Francisco: Ignatius Press, 2008).

26–28]).[10] Polonius is a blithering idiot whose philosophy is blithering idiocy; Macbeth is a bloody murderer whose philosophy is contemptuous of life; Iago is a hate-filled misanthrope whose philosophy is full of hatred toward his fellow man. The very fact that Shakespeare puts these philosophies into the minds and hearts of such despicable characters is a strong indication that he found the philosophies as despicable as the characters.

It is thought that the physical model for the character of Othello might have been the Moorish ambassador of the king of Barbary, who had paid a prolonged visit to Queen Elizabeth's court in 1600 and 1601. The ambassador and his Muslim retinue attracted much attention for their exotic behavior and were naturally described as "Barbarians". A portrait of the ambassador painted during his visit, and inscribed "*Legatus regis barbariae in Angliam*", is valuable for its representation of the ethnic type that Shakespeare probably visualized for his Moorish hero. The ambassador is clearly white-skinned with a dark beard. The fact that the Bard used the "Barbarian" ambassador as the inspiration for the characterization of Othello is suggested still further by Iago's tasteless comment to Brabantio that "you'll have your daughter cover'd with a Barbary horse" (1.1.112–13). This connection between Othello and the Barbary Coast is crucial to our understanding of the ethnicity of Shakespeare's hero because it indicates that Othello would not have been black, but rather a white-skinned Arab. As such, any racism would be more akin to anti-Semitism, in the broader sense of the word "Semitic", than to a prejudice against blacks. It should also be borne in mind that references to a black complexion in Shakespeare's works do

---

[10] *Macbeth*, ed. Joseph Pearce, Ignatius Critical Editions (San Francisco: Ignatius Press, 2010).

not indicate a black face, in the sense that we understand it. Englishmen were regularly described as having a black complexion if they had black hair or dark eyes. Thus, for instance, Sir Griffin Markham, who was imprisoned and facing execution at the time that Shakespeare was writing *Othello*, is described in a contemporary document as having "a large broad face, black complexion ... big nose, and one of his hands maimed by a hurt in his arm received by shot of bullet". The same document describes Sir Griffin's brothers as being "tall of stature, of exceeding swarthy and bad complexion and all hav[ing] very great noses".[11]

Having discussed the demonic Iago and the noble but fatally flawed Othello, it is time to turn our attention to the doomed damsel, Desdemona. Is she as pure and chaste as many critics seem to believe? Does she warrant comparison with the Blessed Virgin, as the critic Peter Milward suggests?[12] Is she as immaculate as the Virgin and as blameless as the Virgin's Son, a spotless victim of the sins of others? In order to answer these questions, we need to begin with the reasons for her initial attraction to Othello. It is not his courtesy that attracts her, still less his practice of Christian virtue; it is the tales he tells of his adventures on the high seas and in strange lands:

> I spake of most disastrous chances,
> Of moving accidents by flood and field,
> Of hairbreadth scapes i' th' imminent deadly breach;
> Of being taken by the insolent foe
> And sold to slavery; of my redemption thence
> And portance in my traveler's history;

[11] Quoted in David Mathew, *Catholicism in England: 1535–1935* (London: Catholic Book Club, 1938), p. 62.

[12] Peter Milward, *Shakespeare's Meta-drama: Othello and King Lear* (Tokyo: Renaissance Institute, 2003), p. 30.

Wherein of antres vast and deserts idle,
Rough quarries, rocks, hills whose heads touch heaven,
It was my hint to speak—such was my process;
And of the Cannibals that each other eat,
The Anthropophagi, and men whose heads
Do grow beneath their shoulders. This to hear
Would Desdemona seriously incline;
But still the house affairs would draw her thence;
Which ever as she could with haste dispatch,
She'd come again, and with a greedy ear
Devour up my discourse.

(1.3.134–50)

Compare these words with those of the Prince of Morocco in *The Merchant of Venice*, who could be seen as a preliminary sketch of Othello:

By this scimitar,
That slew the Sophy, and a Persian prince
That won three fields of Sultan Solyman,
I would o'erstare the sternest eyes that look,
Outbrave the heart most daring on the earth,
Pluck the young sucking cubs from the she-bear,
Yea, mock the lion when 'a roars for prey,
To win [thee], lady.

(2.1.24–31)[13]

Both Moorish characters delight in the boastful telling of their own adventures, and both are ultimately defeated by the blindness of their pride—Morocco in the choosing of the wrong casket, and Othello in the destructive denouement of the tragedy that his pride and jealousy unleash. Note, however, the difference in Portia's response

[13] *The Merchant of Venice*, ed. Joseph Pearce, Ignatius Critical Editions (San Francisco: Ignatius Press, 2009).

to that of Desdemona. Portia, endowed with her father's wisdom, wishes Morocco a "gentle riddance" after he has made his hasty and crestfallen departure (2.7.78), whereas Desdemona, spurning her own father, hangs on to every boastful word, devouring Othello's vaunts "with a greedy ear". It is furthermore Desdemona and not Othello who makes the initial and decisive seductive move, as Othello relates in his defense:

> She thank'd me,
> And bade me, if I had a friend that lov'd her,
> I should but teach him how to tell my story,
> And that would woo her. Upon this hint I spake:
> She lov'd me for the dangers I had pass'd,
> And I lov'd her that she did pity them.
>
> (1.3.163–68)

Desdemona's father, shocked by Othello's account and reluctant to believe that his daughter would "confess that she was half the wooer" (1.3.175), asks her to explain herself:

> Come hither, gentle mistress.
> Do you perceive in all this noble company
> Where most you owe obedience?
>
> (1.3.177–79)

Desdemona's response cuts him to the quick:

> My noble father,
> I do perceive here a divided duty.
> To you I am bound for life and education;
> My life and education both do learn me
> How to respect you; you are the lord of duty—
> I am hitherto your daughter; but here's my husband,
> And so much duty as my mother show'd

To you, preferring you before her father,
So much I challenge that I may profess
Due to the Moor, my lord.

(1.3.180–89)

On first perusal, Desdemona's words seem reasonable
enough. Indeed, they remind us of the words of Cordelia
to her own father, King Lear. There is, however, a crucial
difference between the self-sacrificial dignity and integrity
of Cordelia's words and those of Desdemona. Cordelia has
nothing to gain personally and everything to lose. She sacrifices herself in silent love for her father, suffering exile
for her pains. Desdemona has gained the husband that she
desires and sacrifices her father's feelings in her decision to
elope with the Moor.

Desdemona acts rashly and recklessly, blundering
naïvely into an ultimately abusive marriage that will lead
to her death. The fact is that she is not a good judge of
character. When asked by Emilia if her husband was not
jealous, she replies with an innocence that is tainted by a
degree of ignorance: "Who, he? I think the sun where
he was born / Drew all such humours from him" (3.4.27–
28). Her hopeless naïveté is accentuated by the immediate
arrival of a heatedly jealous Othello. Such weakness on
Desdemona's part plays right into the hands of the fiendish
Iago, as he himself tells us:

Thus credulous fools are caught;
And many worthy and chaste dames even thus,
All guiltless, meet reproach.

(4.1.45–47)

Although the credulous fool to whom Iago refers is
Othello, who too readily believes the worst of his wife,

and although Desdemona is indeed "guiltless" of the sin of infidelity of which she stands accused, she is herself guilty of credulity in her believing of the fantastic yarns that Othello spun about his past adventures, including his tales of men whose heads grow beneath their shoulders, and is credulous in the extreme in eloping with a man whom she hardly knows on the strength of his tales of derring-do.

Unlike Cordelia, who is indeed a blameless victim, Desdemona is at least partially culpable for her own death, as is evident in her last fateful and fatal encounter with Othello. Her last request of her husband as he prepares to smother her is that she should be permitted to say one final prayer. He refuses but, as he suffocates her, she utters the simplest of prayers: "O lord, Lord, Lord!" (5.2.8). For a Catholic in the audience, these words would resonate with the *Domine, non sum dignus* (Lord, I am not worthy) in the Mass, the prayer of contrition repeated three times by the communicant immediately before receiving Communion: *Domine,... Domine,... Domine* (Lord,... Lord,... Lord). The connection with the Mass in this crucial and climactic scene is also evident in Desdemona's twice repeating of the prayer "Have mercy on me" (5.2.36 and 5.2.59), reminiscent of the *misere nobis* (have mercy on us) repeated twice during the *Agnus Dei* (Lamb of God), and is also suggested by Othello's infernal suggestion that his killing of Desdemona is not a murder but a sacrifice. Desdemona's role in this symbolic shadowing of the Mass is, therefore, partly that of Christ, who is sacrificed for a sin He did not commit, but also that of the repentant sinner preparing to receive Christ in Communion. She is guiltless of the sin of adultery for which she is killed but is culpable for her betrayal of her father and the recklessness inherent in her elopement. This is made manifest in her final words:

> *Desdemona.* A guiltless death I die.
> *Emilia.* O, who hath done this deed?
> *Desdemona.* Nobody. I myself. Farewell.
> Commend me to my kind lord. O, farewell! *[She dies.]*
> (5.2.125–28)

On the one hand, Desdemona is reiterating her innocence of the sin of which she stands accused; on the other hand, she states that she herself has done the deed—that is, that she is responsible for her death. Is this, as is often presumed, one last act of loyalty to the husband who has killed her? If so, she is, as Othello proclaims, "like a liar gone to burning hell" because, as he readily confesses or boasts, " 'Twas I that kill'd her" (5.1.132–33). And what do we make of the adjective "kind" being applied to her lord? Surely, this can apply only in an acerbically ironic sense to the man who has just been raging at her, accusing her of adultery, and brutally and fatally attacking her. Yet there is nothing in Desdemona's character to suggest that she is capable of such vitriol. It is out of character. This being so, might her words refer to her other lord, the one whom she had betrayed in eloping with Othello? Is the "kind lord" to whom she wishes to be commended her own father? Such a conclusion is strengthened by the use of the adjective because "kind" has its etymological roots in "kin"—that is, family. In this sense, her father is "kind" whereas Othello is not. Such a reading is suggested by the arrival shortly afterward of Gratiano, Brabantio's brother and Desdemona's uncle, who brings news of Brabantio's death, proclaiming it to Desdemona's corpse:

Poor Desdemona! I am glad thy father's dead.
Thy match was mortal to him, and pure grief
Shore his old thread in atwain. Did he live now,
This sight would make him do a desperate turn,
Yea, curse his better angel from his side,
And fall to reprobance.

(5.2.207–12)

The play's blameless victim is, therefore, not Desdemona but Brabantio, the loving father and "kind lord" who died of a broken heart after his daughter's desertion of him. This being so, it is an error to place Desdemona in the illustrious company of Shakespeare's noble and saintly heroines. She does not belong with Cordelia, a truly blameless victim, or with the sagaciously irrepressible Portia. Instead, she should be placed alongside Shakespeare's tragic heroines who fall through a fatal flaw in their character or through the bad choices they make. She belongs with the impetuously passionate Juliet or with the hopelessly weak Ophelia. We can feel great sympathy for her plight, but we cannot exonerate her totally from the predicament in which she finds herself.

The foregoing line of reasoning as the authentic means of understanding the play's overarching moral and meaning is reinforced by the final lines of Othello before he takes his own life:

I pray you, in your letters,
When you shall these unlucky deeds relate,
Speak of me as I am; nothing extenuate,
Nor set down aught in malice. Then must you speak
Of one that lov'd not wisely but too well;
Of one not easily jealous, but, being wrought,
Perplexed in the extreme; of one whose hand,
Like the base Indian, threw a pearl away
Richer than all his tribe; one of whose subdu'd eyes,

Albeit unused to the melting mood,
Drop tears as fast as the Arabian trees
Their med'cinable gum. Set you down this:
And say besides that in Aleppo once,
Where a malignant and a turban'd Turk
Beat a Venetian and traduc'd the state
I took by th' throat the circumcised dog,
And smote him—thus. [*He stabs himself.*]

(5.2.343–59)

One of the tragic mistakes made in the understanding of this tragedy can be found in the failure to read this speech in its entirety. All too often the accentuation of Othello's description of himself as "one that lov'd not wisely but too well" has been allowed to eclipse the other things he is saying in the moments before his suicide. These words, among the most famous in all of Shakespeare's works, have been allowed to define Othello's character. It is as though we have allowed our understanding of the tragic hero, and by extension the whole tragedy of which he is a part, to be governed by his own final words of self-justification. Yet, as the critic Robert B. Hellman has argued, this line is itself an example of the arrogance at the heart of Othello's character:

In trying to win approval, from others and himself, Othello includes in his summation a one-line definition of himself which has been remembered better than any other part of his apologia—as "one that lov'd not wisely, but too well". Was his vice really an excess of virtue? Or should he have said "not wisely, nor enough"? One can guess that the constant quest of assurance might mean less a free giving of self than a taking for self.[14]

---

[14] Robert B. Hellman, *Magic in the Web: Action and Language in Othello* (Lexington: University of Kentucky Press, 1956); quoted in Oscar James Campbell and Edward G. Quinn, eds., *The Reader's Encyclopedia of Shakespeare* (New York: MJF Books, 1966), p. 607.

For a Christian, and it is perilous to our understanding of the plays to forget that Shakespeare is a Christian, love is always the laying down of the life of the lover for the sake of the beloved. Love is always to die to oneself so that one can give oneself fully to the other. In this sense, Othello never loved Desdemona. On the contrary, in an infernal inversion of the true meaning of love, Othello lays down the life of his beloved for the sake of his own jealousy, sacrificing her on the altar of his own prideful anger. This is not love but its opposite.

Having seen the irony inherent in Othello's prideful efforts to justify himself, we can appreciate the irony of the rest of his final speech. It is, for example, absurd that he states immediately after his claim that he "lov'd too well" that he is "one not easily jealous". He does appear to show true remorse, however, in his lament that he is "one whose hand, / Like the base Indian, threw a pearl away / Richer than all his tribe." These lines are even more poignant if we follow the First Folio edition of the play, published in 1623, only a year after the first publication of the quarto edition, the latter of which is the text used here. The First Folio has "Judean" instead of "Indian", suggesting that Othello is connecting himself to the archtraitor Judas or perhaps to Herod the Great, who had his wife killed in a fit of jealousy.

And what are we to make of the very last lines that Othello utters before fatally stabbing himself?

> Set you down this:
> And say besides that in Aleppo once,
> Where a malignant and a turban'd Turk
> Beat a Venetian and traduc'd the state,
> I took by th' throat the circumcised dog,
> And smote him—thus. [*He stabs himself.*]
> (5.2.354–59)

These lines, so often ignored as being of little importance, are actually crucial to our understanding of the tragedy's denouement, as John Holloway explains:

> [Othello] sees that he has not lived like a Venetian, but like a savage; and the idea leads him to the anecdote which, by its intense ironic charge, offers the final comment upon what he has done, offers a decisive comprehension of it. He has seen that the Turk, chief enemy of Venice, and the Moor, have become one. The "circumcised dog" is himself. For what has Othello done in the case of Desdemona, daughter of a Senator, but "beat a Venetian and traduce the state"?[15]

Thus, in smiting himself he is smiting the enemy of Venice and rendering belated justice to Brabantio for the wrong he has done him in eloping with his daughter and of course rendering justice to Desdemona for his spilling of her innocent blood.

Lest we should miss the point, the final words of the play, spoken by Lodovico, a kinsman of Brabantio, illustrate that justice is done by bestowing Othello's fortune to Brabantio's heir, his brother Gratiano:

> Gratiano, keep the house,
> And seize upon the fortunes of the Moor,
> For they succeed on you. To you, Lord Governor,
> Remains the censure of this hellish villain;
> The time, the place, the torture—O, enforce it!
> Myself will straight aboard; and to the state
> This heavy act with heavy heart relate.
>
> (5.2.368–74)

---

[15] John Holloway, "Othello", in *The Story of the Night: Studies in Shakespeare's Major Tragedies* (London: Routledge and Kegan Paul, 1961), p. 56.

Justice having been done through the confiscation of Othello's goods in compensation for his crime against Desdemona and Brabantio, the play ends with our attention being turned one last time to the "hellish villain", Iago, the play's Machiavellian diabolos for whom no pity or sympathy is warranted.

In this darkest of tragedies, Shakespeare censures the age in which he lives, "the time, the place, the torture", with a tale of darkness, told and tolled with the doom-laden and crushing weight of the playwright's own heavy heart.

Chapter Five

Macbeth

Macbeth, a tragedy of errors, is the shortest play that Shakespeare wrote apart from *The Comedy of Errors*. At only 2,107 lines, it is barely half the length of *Hamlet*, which it rivals in popularity and with which it is often compared. The date of its composition is not certain, but certain clues within the text suggest strongly that it was first performed in 1606. In particular, the discussion of "equivocation" seems to be an allusion to the trial of the Jesuit Henry Garnet, who was executed in May 1606 for his alleged complicity in the Gunpowder Plot of the previous year.[1] The play was written and first performed, therefore, in the wake of one of the most notorious episodes in English history, an event that is still commemorated in England on November 5 each year as Guy Fawkes Night or bonfire night.

The Gunpowder Plot was a foiled attempt by militant and disaffected Catholics, distraught at the increase in persecution during the second year of King James' reign. The plot involved killing the king and his ministers by igniting gunpowder during the state opening of Parliament on November 5, 1605. Scholars such as Antonia Fraser, Hugh Ross Williamson, and others have shown that the angry Catholics who became involved in the infamous plot, such as Robert Catesby and Guy Fawkes, were the dupes of

---

[1] Garnet's defense of "equivocation" formed a major part of his trial.

the Machiavellian machinations of Sir Robert Cecil, son of the infamous Lord Burghley, and his network of spies. The plot may not have been instigated by Cecil, but there seems ample evidence to suggest that he knew about it well in advance and, through the deployment of his spies and *agents provocateurs*, it was always doomed to failure. Instead of leading to an ending of anti-Catholic repression, as its hotheaded organizers had hoped, the ill-conceived scheme played into the hands of Cecil and his cohorts who were seeking to persuade the king to increase the persecution of England's "papists". In the wake of the plot, Catholics found themselves being victimized more brutally and mercilessly than ever.

Shakespeare was related through his mother's family to Robert Catesby, the ringleader of the plotters, and many of Catesby's co-conspirators came from the area of England in which Shakespeare's own family lived. Considering the tight-knit Catholic community of which his family was a part, it seems likely that Shakespeare was acquainted to some degree with several of those involved in the plot. There is, however, no reason to assume that he did not share the horror of most Englishmen, Catholic or Protestant, at this planned act of terrorism. The whole hideous affair was too close to home, and too close for comfort, and it is not surprising that Shakespeare sought to distance himself from those involved.

Although the aforementioned allusion to Garnet's "equivocation" offers evidence of this desire to distance himself from the militant madness of the Gunpowder Plot, it does not necessarily mean that he was showing unquestioning or uncritical support for the king. On the contrary, Stephen Greenblatt expresses surprise that *Macbeth* contains no obvious support for the king in the aftermath of the foiled attempt on his life:

In the wake of the national near catastrophe and the last-minute redemption, it is surprising that the text of *Macbeth* does not contain so much as a prologue, written to the king, celebrating the recent escape; or a complimentary allusion to James's role as the special enemy of Satan and the beloved of God; or a grateful acknowledgment of the happiness of being ruled by Banquo's wise heir.[2]

Andrew Hadfield, in *Shakespeare and Renaissance Politics*, insists that it is "hard to read *Macbeth* and *King Lear* as works that simply accept and reinforce James's beliefs". Furthermore, Hadfield contends, "it would be a mistake to suggest that belonging to the King's Men and performing works at court meant a straightforward acceptance of the King's political beliefs was a necessary prerequisite for such worldly success."[3] There was, in fact, a "culture of lively critical debate" in court literature and "the assumption that plays that dramatized issues close to the royal heart were automatically sycophantic and simply reproduced or expanded the monarch's ideas is wholly at odds with the reality of early modern English drama".[4] The King's Men, Shakespeare's acting troupe, had recently produced Ben Jonson's controversial play, *Sejanus His Fall*, which was known to have provoked the king. Hadfield summarizes the difference between Shakespeare's attitude toward the monarchy during the reign of Elizabeth and his attitude during the reign of James:

Shakespeare's plays written after 1603 concentrate far less on the legitimacy of the monarch than his earlier works

---

[2] Stephen Greenblatt, *Will in the World: How Shakespeare Became Shakespeare* (New York: W. W. Norton, 2004), p. 339.

[3] Andrew Hadfield, *Shakespeare and Renaissance Politics* (London: Arden Shakespeare, 2004), pp. 188–89.

[4] Ibid., p. 189.

had done, and far more on the behaviour of the monarch as a ruler in office. In doing so they are generally simultaneously more supportive of monarchy as an institution and equally—if not more—critical of the monarch's conduct.[5]

Many people had questioned the legitimacy of Elizabeth, who was born of Henry VIII's adulterous relationship with Anne Boleyn, arguing that Henry was still legally married to his first wife, Catharine of Aragon, at the time of Elizabeth's birth. In May 1533, when Anne Boleyn was already visibly pregnant with Elizabeth, Henry had induced Thomas Cranmer to pronounce the nullification of his marriage to Catharine. Since, however, the annulment of his marriage had already been refused by the pope, many considered Cranmer's "nullification" itself null and void and, in consequence, considered Elizabeth a bastard, born out of wedlock, and therefore disqualified from the right of succession to the throne. This was apparently Shakespeare's position, as is clear from his preoccupation with questions of legitimacy in the Elizabethan plays. Ironically, upon his marriage to Jane Seymour, Henry would himself declare Elizabeth illegitimate.

If Shakespeare's preoccupation with legitimacy in his Elizabethan plays suggests his skepticism concerning Elizabeth's legitimacy, his depiction of the role of the monarchy in his Jacobean plays offers strong evidence of his Christian political philosophy. If, as Hadfield surmises, the plays written after James' accession "are generally simultaneously more supportive of monarchy as an institution and equally—if not more—critical of the monarch's conduct", it shows Shakespeare's position vis-à-vis the heated politics of the day. At one extreme, the Puritans were opposed

[5] Ibid.

to monarchy per se, seeking its overthrow and abolition; at the other extreme, James argued for the Divine Right of Kings, insisting that subjects must obey the monarch regardless of his character and the consequences of his actions.[6] Although James believed that kings should rule justly, he argued that unjust kings must still be obeyed regardless of the crimes they commit. He insisted that the king was "Gods Lieutenant in earth" and, as such, is "master over every person that inhabiteth the same, having power over the life and death of every one of them":[7]

> The wickedness therefore of the King can never make them that are ordained to be judged by him, to become his Judges.... A wicked king is sent by God for a curse to his people, and a plague for their sinnes: but that it is lawfull to them to shake off that curse at their owne hand, which God hath laid on them, that I deny, and may do so justly.[8]

In the context of these two extremes of political philosophy, Shakespeare's position can be seen as a *via media* in which monarchy is defended as valid but is seen as being subservient to Christian moral precepts that the monarch has no right to violate. This had been the position of Sir Thomas More, who could not support King Henry VIII when he declared himself head of the Church in

---

[6] In 1642, only twenty-six years after Shakespeare's death, England would be plunged into a bloody civil war in which these two extremes fought for supremacy. The victory of Cromwell's Puritan forces over those of King Charles I led to the abolition of the monarchy and the establishment of a short-lived Commonwealth. The monarchy was restored in 1660.

[7] James I, *The Trew Law of Free Monarchies*, in *The Workes* (London: Robert Barker and John Bull, 1616; facsimile, Hildesheim: Georg Olms Verlag, 1971), p. 203.

[8] Ibid., p. 206.

England because the king was usurping powers that were not rightfully his. Declaring that he was the king's good servant, but God's first, More suffered martyrdom rather than accept the king's usurpation of power. It is this "subsidiarist" understanding of the nature and power of monarchy that informs the plays of Shakespeare. In particular, *Macbeth* presents two starkly different visions of kingship, one of which is rooted in the medieval understanding of kingship, the other in the new cynical pragmatism of Machiavelli's *Prince*. Those who follow the former, represented in the play by the Scottish King Duncan and his son Malcolm, and by the English king, St. Edward the Confessor, consider themselves subject to the moral imperative of living and ruling in obedience to Christian virtue; those who follow the latter, represented by Macbeth, usurp authentic authority through the malevolent employment of Machiavellian realpolitik in defiance of Christian virtue. Furthermore, both types of kingship rely on supernatural power—the former receiving miraculous grace; the latter, self-deceiving demonic temptation. The extent to which Shakespeare saw King James as being represented in the play by the virtuous monarchs or by their diabolical counterpart is an intriguing metadramatic subplot worthy of further examination. Such an investigation must begin with the probable sources on which the Bard relied for the major elements of his play.

Most of the ingredients that Shakespeare threw into the inspirational cauldron of his Scottish potboiler are to be found in Holinshed's *Chronicles of England, Scotlande and Irelande*, published in 1577, a work that is clearly the principal source for *Macbeth* as it is the principal source for many of Shakespeare's other plays. Although other histories of Scotland were available, Shakespeare would have needed to look no further than Holinshed for the key facts of Macbeth's life. It is, however, likely that a sinister episode in the life of King James also contributed as a source of Shakespeare's inspiration.

In August 1600, three years before his accession to the English throne, James, as king of Scotland, visited Gowrie House, the estate of the Earl of Gowrie. According to the official account, the king was lured by Alexander, the earl's brother, into a turret of the castle. The king's retinue, not knowing his whereabouts, were about to set out from the castle to search for him when they were startled by the sight of James leaning from a window of the turret, screaming, "I am murdered! Treason!" One of the king's men ascended the staircase to the turret and found James still struggling with his assailant. Alexander Gowrie was stabbed to death, as was his brother, the Earl of Gowrie. As news of the incident spread, James' government embellished the story by claiming that the Earl of Gowrie was not only a traitor who had sought to murder the king, violating his obligations as a host, but that he was also in league with the devil. It was disclosed that a "little close parchment bag, full of magical characters and words of enchantment," was found on his body at his death and that it was only after this bag of sorcery was removed that the earl's body began to bleed from its wounds. The bag's Hebrew inscription proved that the Earl of Gowrie was a "cabbalist, a studier of magic, and a conjurer of devils". A witch hunt ensued of those alleged to have been co-conspirators and, under severe interrogation using a torture device known as the "boot", which crushed the bones of the feet, a full flurry of "confessions" was obtained, quickly followed by the execution of those deemed "guilty" of taking part in the cabbalistic conspiracy against His Majesty.[9]

---

[9] The Gowrie conspiracy is discussed in Greenblatt, *Will in the World*, pp. 340–41. Greenblatt's source is Louis Barbé, *The Tragedy of Gowrie House* (London: Alexander Gardner, 1887).

Although few dared to question the official line of inquiry about the "conspiracy", many suspected foul play on the king's part. Rather than the king being the victim of a treasonable conspiracy, it was widely believed that he had been its perpetrator. Two powerful nobles whom the king distrusted and to whom he was eighty thousand pounds in debt had been killed, conveniently removing both the nobles and the debt in one murderous stroke, and, to add insult to injury, the king's final Machiavellian *coup de grâce* was the seizure of the Gowrie estate as "compensation".

In the wake of the trial and execution of the "Gowrie conspirators", Scottish ministers were commanded "to praise God for the King's miraculous delivery from that vile treason". Although most complied, however reluctantly, several refused to do so, unwilling in conscience to be guilty by association with the suspected foul deed, or of making a sinful prayer of "praise" for its success. These conscientious objectors suffered the consequence of acting according to their Christian principles by being summarily dismissed from their posts.

What did Shakespeare think about the intricacies of this morbid and macabre saga, a saga that seems to foreshadow the grotesque and grisly plot of *Macbeth*? Was this modern-day horror story as much a part of the dark imaginative backdrop to his Scottish play as the distant history that is the play's ostensible theme? Contemporary evidence suggests that it was.

In 1604, a playwright affiliated with Shakespeare's acting troupe, the King's Men, wrote a play based upon the Gowrie conspiracy. This was itself a risky undertaking because Queen Elizabeth, in 1559, at the very beginning of her reign, had banned all plays about contemporary religious or political issues. All of Shakespeare's plays were written under this law of censorship, which is why they are set in the past or in foreign countries, separated from the hot topics of Elizabethan and Jacobean England by the dramatic distance of time or space. Much of the timeless dimension of Shakespeare's work is due to this legally enforced avoidance of the purely topical issues of his own time. Such "avoidance" does not mean that the plays lacked contemporary relevance or that they were silent on the political and religious controversies of his day (quite the contrary), but it did necessitate a degree of prudential discretion, decorum, and circumspection that has led to this dimension being less discernible than would otherwise have been the case. The advantage is that Shakespeare's works are far more readily accessible to later generations than the works of writers such as Jonathan Swift, John Dryden, Alexander Pope, or even Dante, whose satirical engagement with the issues of their own time has rendered their works more difficult for future generations to comprehend. The disadvantage is that Shakespeare's commentary on the issues of his own time can be fathomed only by diligent detective work on the part of later generations, and, when such detective work is deficient or defective, the contemporary meaning of the plays is lost. Although it is true, as Ben Jonson mused, that Shakespeare is "not of an age, but for all time", it is ironic that part of the reason is that his own age would not let him speak openly of it!

Why, then, did a playwright affiliated with the King's Men seek to write a play on the Gowrie conspiracy, an event that happened only four years earlier and that was not only contemporary but controversial? Was this mysterious playwright Shakespeare himself? And what did the play say about the conspiracy? Did it accept the king's "official" version that the aim of the conspiracy was his own assassination, or did it hint at a darker duplicity at work behind the scenes? It is, of course, inconceivable that the play should accuse the king of treachery directly, even if the playwright suspected him of it, since not only would such a play be banned, but the playwright would find himself in prison, perhaps en route to the gallows. Shakespeare's friend Ben Jonson had already found himself in prison, seven years earlier, following his writing of a play that had committed the crime of satirizing Queen Elizabeth's government. It is unlikely that the writer of the play on the Gowrie conspiracy would commit the same indiscretion. Perhaps, as Stephen Greenblatt has surmised, the play was written to test whether the censorship imposed by Elizabeth would still be enforced under James.[10] In any event, the play, *The Tragedy of Gowrie*, was twice performed before large crowds in December 1604 before being apparently banned by the censors. The reason for the banning of the play was evident in a contemporary report that hints at James' discomfort at its being performed: "Whether the matter or manner be not handled well, or that it be thought unfit that Princes should be played on the Stage in their Life-time, I hear that some great Councilors are much displeased with it, and so 'tis thought it shall be forbidden."[11] The play has not survived, so it is impossible to know how the unknown playwright handled the controversy surrounding the conspiracy. It is, however, clear that James was not happy with it, suggesting perhaps that his own role in the sordid affair was not something on which he wished to dwell. Whether or not "it be thought unfit that Princes should be played on the Stage in their Life-time", it was perhaps the case

---

[10] Greenblatt, *Will in the World*, p. 341.

[11] Ibid. Greenblatt does not provide the original source for this quote, and his bibliographical notes do not indicate the title of the work from which he obtained it.

that Machiavellian Princes did not want reminding of the "unfit" parts they had played in real-life events. As Macbeth reminds us: "False face must hide what the false heart doth know" (1.7.82). Had the unknown writer of *The Tragedy of Gowrie* succeeded in exposing King James in the same manner in which Hamlet had exposed King Claudius with the staging of *The Mousetrap*, the play within a play: "the play's the thing / Wherein I'll catch the conscience of the king"? (2.2.600–601).[12] Had the king's conscience been pricked, provoking the banning of the play?

Although no definitive answer can be given to the foregoing questions, it is surely reasonable to see a connection between this earlier Scottish play, with which Shakespeare was almost certainly involved, either as its writer or as one of the actors of the King's Men who performed it, and the other Scottish play on which Shakespeare began to work almost immediately afterward. If this is so, it is difficult to see the sinister conspiracies unfolding in *Macbeth* without seeing the shadow of the Gowrie conspiracy looming ominously in the background. In order to illustrate this more clearly, it is necessary to perceive the circumstances surrounding Shakespeare's writing of *Macbeth*.

As already stated, there is no evidence that Shakespeare sympathized with the violent idealism of the Gunpowder Plotters, and it is likely that he shared the abhorrence of such extremism felt by most people, Catholics and Protestants alike. Yet he would surely have shared the sense of desolation at the renewal of the persecution, following as it did so soon after the initial exhilaration of the queen's death and the king's accession. Nor was Shakespeare's own family immune from the renewed persecution. As noted, his daughter Susanna was fined in Stratford as a

---

[12] *Macbeth*, ed. Joseph Pearce, Ignatius Critical Editions (San Francisco: Ignatius Press, 2010). Text references are to act, scene, and line.

Catholic recusant in May 1606, the same month in which the Jesuit Henry Garnet was executed in London for his alleged involvement in the Gunpowder Plot, and around the time that Shakespeare is believed to have been working on *Macbeth*.

As Shakespeare worked on the new Scottish play that would rise, phoenixlike, from the ashes of the banned *Tragedy of Gowrie*, his hopes of a new dawn of religious and political freedom were seemingly lying in irreparable tatters. This sense of all-pervasive darkness broods over *Macbeth* as it broods over the other plays he wrote during this period. As he sat down in the dark days of 1606 to write this darkest of tragedies, one can imagine the sense of desolate anger with which he wrote. Somehow, without incriminating himself or having his new play share the fate of *The Tragedy of Gowrie*, he sought to vent his spleen against the Machiavellian monarch. As Hildegard Hammerschmidt-Hummel surmised: "Shakespeare's inspiration for the character of Macbeth was—as it appears—not so much the historical figure of the medieval Scottish king, as James I himself."[13]

This explosively charged backdrop to Shakespeare's writing of the play helps to explain the bleak and desolate atmosphere that looms like an oppressive cloud over the drama itself. This darkness was evoked with particular eloquence by the Shakespeare scholar A. C. Bradley:

A Shakespearean tragedy, as a rule, has a special tone or atmosphere of its own, quite perceptible, however difficult to describe. The effect of this atmosphere is marked with unusual strength in *Macbeth*.... Darkness, we may even

---

[13] Hildegard Hammerschmidt-Hummel, *The Life and Times of William Shakespeare 1564–1616* (London: Chaucer Press, 2007), p. 260.

say blackness, broods over this tragedy. It is remarkable
that almost all the scenes which at once recur to memory take place either at night or in some dark spot. The
vision of the dagger, the murder of Duncan, the murder
of Banquo, the sleep-walking of Lady Macbeth, all come
in night-scenes. The Witches dance in the thick air of a
storm, or, "black and midnight hags," receive Macbeth in
a cavern. The blackness of night is to the hero a thing of
fear, even of horror; and that which he feels becomes the
spirit of the play. The faint glimmerings of the western
sky at twilight are here menacing: it is the hour when the
traveller hastens to reach safety in his inn, and when Banquo rides homeward to meet his assassins; the hour when
"light thickens," when "night's black agents to their prey
do rouse," when the wolf begins to howl, and the owl
to scream, and withered murder steals forth to his work.
Macbeth bids the stars hide their fires that his "black"
desires may be concealed; Lady Macbeth calls on thick
night to come, palled in the dunnest smoke of hell. The
moon is down and no stars shine when Banquo, dreading
the dreams of the coming night, goes unwillingly to bed,
and leaves Macbeth to wait for the summons of the little
bell. When the next day should dawn, its light is "stran-
gled," and "darkness does the face of earth entomb." In
the whole drama the sun seems to shine only twice: first,
in the beautiful but ironical passage where Duncan sees
the swallows flitting round the castle of death; and, after-
wards, when at the close the avenging army gathers to rid
the earth of its shame.[14]

As always, the "delirious" atmosphere of Shakespeare's
plots, to which Chesterton draws our attention, is seen to
have its source in the unremitting darkness of the times in

[14] A. C. Bradley, *Shakespearean Tragedy: Lectures on Hamlet, Othello, King Lear,
Macbeth* (London: Macmillan, 1905), pp. 333–34.

which the playwright lives, and is manifested in the sort of grotesque nightmare imagery normally associated with Dante's hell:

> Images like those of the babe torn smiling from the breast and dashed to death; of pouring the sweet milk of concord into hell; of the earth shaking in fever; of the frame of things disjointed; of sorrows striking heaven on the face, so that it resounds and yells out like syllables of dolour; of the mind lying in restless ecstasy on a rack; of the mind full of scorpions; of the tale told by an idiot, full of sound and fury;—all keep the imagination moving on a "wild and violent sea," while it is scarcely for a moment permitted to dwell on thoughts of peace and beauty.[15]

Now, having set the scene in which the playwright settles down to write, let's examine the gloomy fruits of his muse.

The play opens in the presence of supernatural evil. The three witches, presaged by a devilish fanfare of thunder and lightning, prophesy their impending meeting with Macbeth in an incantation that connects demonic evil with its human incarnation:

> Fair is foul, and foul is fair:
> Hover through the fog and filthy air.
> (I.I.10–11)

On the demonic level, represented by the witches, evil is the malicious inversion of the good: that which is fair is foul, and that which is foul is fair. Since the good is a manifestation of God, it is hated by the satanic, the enemies of God, and is therefore inverted.[16] Man, represented in

---

[15] Ibid., p. 336.
[16] "Satan" is a Hebrew word meaning "adversary" or "accuser".

this scene by the impending arrival of Macbeth, is made in the image of God and has, therefore, a natural desire for the good. He is not eternally at war with the good, as are the demons, and must be diverted from the good in order to serve evil. Whereas the demonic evil of the witches is a satanic *inversion*, the evil of Macbeth must be the fruit of *perversion*, a consequence of the *diversion* from good prompted by the temptation that the witches will provide. The play's theme is, therefore, revealed in its opening lines as being the perversion of Macbeth, a perversion that is prophesied by satanic forces. Already there is the hint of a connection between this philosophical and theological understanding of evil and its political manifestation in Machiavellian *realpolitik*. It is the Machiavel who believes that evil means can be justified by the "goodness" of the end. If the end is deemed to be "fair", the Machiavel believes himself justified in acting as though fair is foul and foul is fair in the pursuit of the "fairness" of the end. For the Christian, the pursuit of evil means to a good end is illicit, not least because both the end and the person pursuing it are corrupted thereby. This fundamental understanding of political and moral philosophy is at the hub and heart of *Macbeth* and serves as an impassioned admonishment to those such as the Gunpowder Plotters who pursued ostensibly good ends—that is, the overthrow of tyranny—by serving evil means—that is, terrorism. Needless to say, it also serves as a condemnation of Machiavellian monarchs, such as James, who invent "conspiracies" in order to profit thereby.

It is also significant that the play opens with the *objective* presence of supernatural forces. The witches are not the figment of someone else's imagination, because there is nobody else present to witness them. They are alone, and therefore they stand alone, utterly independent. We are in the real presence of evil, an evil that really exists whether we like it or not, and not an evil that is merely the product of our fetid fetishes or our fevered imaginations. In its formal structure, therefore, *Macbeth* places us unequivocally in a supernatural cosmos, rendering implausible all materialistic interpretations of the play's intrinsic meaning.

Having established the supernatural infrastructure upon which the drama depends, we are presented in the following scene with the metaphysical dilemma on which it hangs. To what extent is man a slave to his fate or fortune, or, conversely, to what extent does providence provide the freedom for man to carve out his future, under grace, in terms of the sinfulness or virtue of his actions? The sergeant, reporting the heroic deeds of Macbeth in battle, compares fortune to "a rebel's whore" over which Macbeth triumphs:

> The merciless Macdonwald—
> Worthy to be a rebel, for to that
> The multiplying villainies of nature
> Do swarm upon him. . . .
> . . . .
> And Fortune, on his damned quarrel smiling,
> Show'd like a rebel's whore. But all's too weak;
> For brave Macbeth—well he deserves that name—
> Disdaining Fortune, with his brandish'd steel
> Which smok'd with bloody execution,
> Like valour's minion, carv'd out his passage
> Till he fac'd the slave.
>
> (1.2.9–12, 14–20)

Thus, we see the mighty pinnacle of valor and virtue from which Macbeth will fall. He begins by treating the false promises of fortune, the "rebel's whore", with disdain, and ends as a fool who allows his own rebel heart to be seduced by the whores, all three of them, and whose downfall is due to his believing their lies, damned lies, and half-truths. He begins as the worthy and noble slayer of Macdonwald, a man who deserves the name of "rebel" because of the "multiplying villainies of nature" that "swarm upon him", and ends as an ignominious rebel himself, whose multiplying villainies have swarmed upon him to his own destruction. Macbeth ends by *becoming* Macdonwald, a rebel whose decapitated head is paraded as a symbol of the defeat of evil. Is it, for example, a curious coincidence, or perhaps an example of Shakespeare's unsurpassed genius as a master of structural symmetry, that we are informed of the fixing of Macdonwald's decapitated head on the battlements of the castle twenty-three lines from the beginning of the drama, and are presented with Macbeth's decapitated head twenty-three lines from its conclusion?

We begin to fear the worst for Macbeth when we see how he is so easily seduced by the beguiling prophecies of the witches. Whereas Banquo responds to the witches with a healthy disdain for the fortune they profess to predict, Macbeth seems besotted with the possibilities set forth before him. In the instant before he first sets eyes on the witches, Macbeth echoes their satanic incantation "fair is foul, and foul is fair" with an unwitting judgment of his own: "So foul and fair a day I have not seen" (1.3.38). Although his words are seemingly innocent enough, comparing the foulness of the weather with the fairness of the victory over the rebels, we can't help but hear them as an ominous portent of his doom.

After the witches have vanished into thin air, it is Macbeth who is hungry to learn more. Banquo is altogether more skeptical. Whereas Banquo sees the vision as one of evil, and therefore to be spurned, "disdaining fortune", Macbeth is excited by what he perceives as good news.

He is to be Thane of Cawdor and "King hereafter"!
(1.3.50). No sooner have the prophecies been spoken by
the witches, or weird sisters, than the first of them is confirmed. When Ross arrives to announce that Macbeth has
been made Thane of Cawdor, Banquo asks whether it's
possible for the devil to "speak true" (1.3.107). A few lines
later, in a cautionary aside to Macbeth, he answers his own
question:

> And oftentimes to win us to our harm,
> The instruments of darkness tell us truths.
> Win us with honest trifles, to betray's
> In deepest consequence.
>
> (1.3.123–26)

Macbeth is deaf to such warnings, though they be steeped
in Christian wisdom, and chooses instead to flirt with evil:

> Two truths are told,
> As happy prologues to the swelling act
> Of the imperial theme....
> This supernatural soliciting
> Cannot be ill; cannot be good. If ill,
> Why hath it given me earnest of success,
> Commencing in a truth? I am Thane of Cawdor.
> If good, why do I yield to that suggestion
> Whose horrid image doth unfix my hair
> And make my seated heart knock at my ribs
> Against the use of nature? Present fears
> Are less than horrible imaginings.
> My thought, whose murder yet is but fantastical,
> Shakes so my single state of man
> That function is smother'd in surmise,
> And nothing is but what is not.
>
> (1.3.127–41)

Macbeth's willful blindness, or deafness, is evident from the fact that Banquo had already answered his first question. The "supernatural soliciting" *can* be "ill", even if it gives Macbeth "earnest of success", because, as Banquo says, the "instruments of darkness" will often "tell us truths" in order to "win us to our harm". Even the prospect of becoming king is nothing but a "trifle" compared with the "deepest consequence" of eternal damnation. "For what is a man profited, if he shall gain the whole world, and lose his own soul?"[17] The lines from St. Matthew's Gospel must have resonated with Shakespeare's Christian audience, as must the words of Christ that follow almost immediately afterward: "For the Son of man shall come in the glory of his Father; and then he shall reward every man according to his works."[18] Blinded by ambition, Macbeth does not see the wisdom of the biblical question implicit in Banquo's words, nor the warning of the "deepest consequence" of forgetting that we will be judged or "rewarded" according to our works. Macbeth already prefers the darkness of worldly ambition to the light of Christian wisdom, choosing the lies of the coven to the truth of the Covenant. This is evident from the fact that his lines are spoken as a secretive aside, hidden from the eyes and ears of others. From now on, Macbeth will live increasingly in the narrow and narrowing confines of his own head, making himself the center of his own contracted and constricted cosmos. As he speaks to himself in secret, divorcing himself from others, his subjective perception supersedes objective reality. His decay is, therefore, as much a decay of philosophy as it is a decay of morality. The more he thinks of himself, the less he thinks of others, and the less he thinks of others,

---

[17] Matthew 16:26 (KJV).
[18] Matthew 16:27 (KJV).

the less he thinks of the Other—that is, the truth that transcends the self. The result is that his first thought of murder
coincides with the murder of thought:

> My thought, whose murder yet is but fantastical,
> Shakes so my single state of man
> That function is smother'd in surmise,
> And nothing is but what is not.
>
> (1.3.138–41)

As Macbeth's pride takes pride of place on the throne of
his soul, he begins to lose his sense of reality. Sin smothers
reason so that the normal function of a man's mind, which
is to seek and find the truth, is "smother'd in surmise" until
"nothing is but what is not". Thus, Macbeth's nihilism,
which will come to bitter and futile fruition in the final act
with his dismissal of life as "a tale / Told by an idiot, full of
sound and fury, / Signifying nothing" (5.5.26–28), is seen
to have its roots in the play's opening act with his turning away from *fides et ratio* toward infidelity and irrational-
ity. Macbeth is thus revealed as an anti-Hamlet. Whereas
Hamlet begins in the Slough of Despond, temperamen-
tally tempted to despair, he grows in virtue throughout the
play until he reaches the ripeness of Christian conversion
and the readiness to accept his own death as part of God's
benign providence:

> Not a whit, we defy augury: there is a special providence
> in the fall of a sparrow. If it be now, 'tis not to come; if it
> be not to come, it will be now, if it be not now, yet it will
> come—the readiness is all. Since no man owes of aught he
> leaves, what is't to leave betimes? Let be. (5.2.211–17)[19]

---

[19] *Hamlet*, ed. Joseph Pearce, Ignatius Critical Editions (San Francisco: Ignatius Press, 2008).

Hamlet ends by defying "augury"; Macbeth ends by defying everything except "augury". Hamlet grows in faith *because* he grows in reason; Macbeth loses his faith *because* he loses his reason.

Like Aristotle and St. Thomas Aquinas, Hamlet never loses sight of the distinction between the *essence* of things and their *accidental* qualities. He concerns himself with *definitions*, with the meaning of things, and with the distinction between those things that essentially *are* and those that only *seem* to be. "*Seems*, madam?" says Hamlet to his mother. "Nay, it *is*. I know not 'seems'" (1.2.76; italics added). Hamlet does not make Macbeth's fatal mistake of allowing himself to become "smother'd in surmise", nor does he succumb to Macbeth's irrational despair of believing that life signifies nothing. Hamlet knows that life is about what things *mean*, not what they *seem*, and that the secret of life is learning to discover the difference between the two. Whereas Hamlet knows that life is the quest for the definite amid the clouds of unknowing, Macbeth loses his head and soul in the unknowing clouds of his own sin-deceived ego. Far from seeing life as a quest, Macbeth is left with nothing but his own bitter inquest on life, "signifying nothing". This is the "deepest consequence" of Macbeth's rejection of faith and reason. In losing sight of the significance of others, or the Other, he loses sight of the significance of everything else. In choosing himself above others, he is not even left with himself. He loses everything, even his own soul. He is left with the "nothing" that is nothing else but the real absence of the good that he has rejected. This psychological shrinking was described by G. K. Chesterton, with his usual perspicacity and eloquence, as "the first and most formidable of the great actualities of *Macbeth*":

Make a morbid decision and you will only become more morbid; do a lawlesss thing and you will only get into an atmosphere much more suffocating than that of law. Indeed, it is a mistake to speak of a man as "breaking out." The lawless man never breaks out; he breaks in. He smashes a door and finds himself in another room, he smashes a wall and finds himself in a yet smaller one. The more he shatters the more his habitation shrinks. Where he ends you may read in the end of *Macbeth*.

For us moderns, therefore, the first philosophical significance of the play is this; that our life is one thing and that our lawless acts limit us; every time we break a law we make a limitation. In some strange way hidden in the deeps of human psychology, if we build our palace on some unknown wrong it turns very slowly into our prison. Macbeth at the end of the play is not merely a wild beast; he is a caged wild beast.[20]

[20] G. K. Chesterton, "The Macbeths", first published posthumously in *John o' London's Weekly*, January 5, 1951; republished in G. K. Chesterton, *The Spice of Life* (Beaconsfield: Darwen Finlayson, 1964), pp. 47–48.

Chapter Six

Frankenstein

Mary Shelley's *Frankenstein* is one of the most influential novels of the nineteenth century; it is also one of the most misunderstood and abused. In recent years, it has been vivisected critically by latter-day Victor Frankensteins who have transformed the meanings emergent from the novel into monsters of their own contorted imaginations. Most particularly, Franken feminists have turned the novel into a monster of misanthropy. Seldom has a work of fiction suffered so scandalously from the slings and arrows of outrageous criticism.

Much of the problem in understanding the novel derives from the conflicting forces at work in its pages, forces that were a whirlwind of warring influences in the mind and heart of its teenage author. On a purely emotional level, the young Mary Shelley was surrounded by tragedy, including the death in early infancy of her first child and the suicide of two intimate relations. She was also battling with the monsters of modernity, and struggling with the atheistic philosophy of her father and the iconoclastic musings of her lover. Within the pages of *Frankenstein*, we see the savagery of Rousseau; the pseudo-satanic manipulation of Milton; the Romantic reaction against the "dark satanic mills" of science and industrialism; the conflict between the "light" Romanticism of Wordsworth and Coleridge and the "darker" Romanticism of Byron and Shelley; and, perhaps most enigmatically, the struggle between the two Shelleys themselves, and perhaps the emergence of Mary from Percy's shadow.

Since the personhood of Mary Shelley is daubed across the pages of *Frankenstein* in gaudy shades of angst-driven self-expression, it is crucial to understand something about the author before we can begin to get to grips with the work. In the Preface to the Norton Critical Edition of *Frankenstein*, J. Paul Hunter describes Mary as being "irritated by the torments of conventional family values".[1] Such an assessment is singularly odd considering that Mary had no experience of "conventional family values", her own family and her own upbringing being anything but conventional. Her father, William Godwin, was a proponent of atheism and an advocate of the dissolution of the institution of marriage, describing marriage as "the worst of all laws"; her mother, Mary Wollstonecraft, a proto-feminist, died eleven days after Mary's birth on August 30, 1797, from childbirth complications. In 1801, her father remarried. Thereafter, the "family" in which Mary was raised consisted of her father, her stepmother, a stepbrother and stepsister, and a half sister, Fanny Imlay, the daughter of her mother by Gilbert Imlay. *Pace* Dr. Hunter, any "torments" suffered by Mary Shelley must be laid at the door of her very "unconventional" family background.

In November 1812, Mary, now fifteen years old, met Percy Bysshe Shelley for the first time. He was with Harriet Westbrook, whom he had just married. In July 1814, Percy Shelley deserted his pregnant wife and one-year-old

---

[1] J. Paul Hunter, Preface to *Frankenstein*, by Mary Shelley (New York: W. W. Norton, 1966), p. vii.

child and fled to the Continent with the sixteen-year-old Mary, who was also pregnant. In November, Harriet Shelley gave birth to her second child; in the following February, Mary gave birth, prematurely, to a daughter who died within a few days. Almost a year later, in January 1816, Mary gave birth to a son, William.

In the summer of 1816, Mary and Percy visited Lord Byron at the Villa Diodati by Lake Geneva in Switzerland. After reading *Fantasmagoriana*, an anthology of German ghost stories, Byron challenged Mary, Percy, and his personal physician, John William Polidori, each to compose a story of his own. Byron, responding to his own challenge, began to write about the vampire legends he had heard while traveling in the Balkans. He aborted his attempt to bring the fragment to fruition, but Polidori, using Byron's fragment as inspiration, wrote *The Vampyre*, which, when published in 1819, became the progenitor of the romantic vampire literary genre. Polidori's modest literary achievement would be eclipsed, however, by *Frankenstein*, which was Mary's response to Byron's challenge.

Mary began writing *Frankenstein* in June 1816, when she was still only eighteen years old, and would not finish it until the following May. The eleven months during which she was working on the novel were almost as macabre in real life as was the unfolding of the plot in the teenager's fevered imagination. In October 1816, Fanny Imlay, Mary's half sister, committed suicide, and in December, the drowned body of Harriet Shelley was discovered in the Serpentine, in London's Hyde Park, some weeks after she had presumably committed suicide. On December 30, barely days after the discovery of Harriet's body, Mary and Percy were married in St. Mildred's Church in Bread Street, London. (The church had been selected because Bread Street was where John Milton had been born more than two centuries earlier.) In March 1817, Percy was denied custody of his two children by Harriet. All this happened while Mary was working on *Frankenstein*, and the shadow of these events account, no doubt, for much of the doom-laden and death-darkened atmosphere of the novel. It might almost be said, or at least plausibly suggested, that the ghost of Harriet Shelley haunted the author's imagination as she worked; if so, it is equally plausible to suggest that the Monster can be seen as a metaphor for the destructive power of the unleashed passion between Mary and Percy. Following the same line of deduction, it could be said that Frankenstein's guilt-ridden horror of the destruction he had caused is itself a reflection of Mary's guilt at the consequences of her passionate affair with Shelley. This allegorical reading of the novel would place Mary Shelley in the role of Victor Frankenstein and the Monster in the role of the illicit and destructive relationship between Mary and Percy.

Although the presence of this tragic backdrop pervades the whole work, it should not eclipse the many other elements that serve to add to the doom-laden cocktail of depth and delusion that makes *Frankenstein* such a beguilingly deceptive story. From the very beginning, on the title page itself, we are given tantalizing clues concerning the aesthetic and philosophical roots of Mary Shelley's inspiration and perhaps an inkling of her purpose. In giving *Frankenstein* the alternative title of *The Modern Prometheus*, and coupling it with the epigraph conveying Adam's complaint from *Paradise Lost*, we see the leitmotif established concerning the relationship between Creator, creature, and creativity. The allusion to the Prometheus myth conjures images of the creation of man in defiance of the gods; the citation of Adam's complaint conjures the image of the creation of man in defiance of man:

Did I request thee, Maker, from my clay
To mould me man? Did I solicit thee
From darkness to promote me?[2]

Prometheus presumes to take powers that are not rightfully his in order to create man; Adam presumes to rebuke his Creator for bringing him into existence. It is clear, therefore, that Victor Frankenstein can be seen as a Prometheus figure, and the Monster as a figure of Milton's Adam.

It is important from the outset to distinguish between the biblical Adam and the Adam depicted by Milton in *Paradise Lost*. The two Adams are very different, and it is perilous to conflate them. The biblical Adam does not rebuke his Creator for bringing him into existence; at most he blames Eve for his Fall and implies, in the naked shame of his transgression, that it would have been better if God had not created her to be his mate. He never takes the prideful position of questioning the Creator's wisdom in creating him; still less does he imply the nihilistic option of wishing his own oblivion. On the contrary, it is clear that he remains grateful to God for his existence and grateful for the gift of Eve, in spite of his adolescent defensiveness in the wake of their primal act of disobedience.

Milton's Adam, like Milton's Satan—and, for that matter, Milton's Father and Milton's Son—is a presumptive product of Milton's own theological prejudices, divorced from orthodox tradition. It should be remembered that Milton's quasi-unitarianism is anathema to Protestants and Catholics alike. His Father appears to be a petty dictator; his Satan a freedom fighter; his Son a mere creature, cold and arrogant, who is created after Satan; and his Holy Spirit conspicuous by His absence. It is, therefore, a

---

[2] John Milton, *Paradise Lost*, bk. 10, lines 743–45.

peculiar Miltonian "Christianity" that serves as a catalyst to Mary Shelley's imagination. Whether she knew it or not, she was not reacting against Christianity per se but against a pseudo-Christian heresy. As such, any reading of *Frankenstein* that purports to see it as an attack on Christian orthodoxy, as understood by Protestants or Catholics, is hopelessly awry.

The importance of Milton to the Romantic poets in general, and to Percy Shelley in particular, is difficult to overstate. Mary and Percy had read *Paradise Lost* together before Mary embarked upon the writing of *Frankenstein*, and Percy's sympathy for Milton's Satan, and his implicit disdain for Milton's God, were evident in his essay "A Defense of Poetry":

> Nothing can exceed the energy and magnificence of the character of Satan as expressed in *Paradise Lost*. It is a mistake to suppose that he could ever have been intended for the popular personification of evil.... Milton's Devil as a moral being is as far superior to his God as one who perseveres in some purpose which he has conceived to be excellent in spite of adversity and torture is to one who in the cold security of undoubted triumph inflicts the most horrible revenge upon his enemy.... Milton has so far violated the popular creed (if this shall be judged to be a violation) as to have alleged no superiority of moral virtue to his God over his Devil. And this bold neglect of a direct moral purpose is the most decisive proof of the supremacy of Milton's genius [over Dante's].[3]

Percy Shelley was also preoccupied with Prometheus, as his later work, "Prometheus Unbound", would testify,

---

[3] Percy Bysshe Shelley, "A Defense of Poetry", in *The Complete Works of Percy Bysshe Shelley*, vol. 7 (London: Ernest Benn Limited, 1965), pp. 129–30.

and we see how Milton's myth and the myth of Prometheus are conflated in *Frankenstein* to serve as the creative catalyst for the cataclysmic plot. The Miltonian-Promethean nexus can be seen to offer a multiplicity of allegorical applicability. Milton's God conflates with Zeus as the minister of divinely deviant injustice (an apt conflation considering that the Miltonian "God the Father" has more in common with the classical "Father of the Gods" than he has with the First Person of the Trinity). Victor Frankenstein can be cast in the role of God (Zeus) as the creator of man (Titan), in which case the Monster is cast in the Miltonian role of Adam (Satan). Such a reading of the novel is legitimate, up to a point, and is, in fact, the preferred allegorical interpretation of many non-Christian or anti-Christian critics, enabling, as it does, an implicitly anti-religious "moral" to emerge from the text (as long as we forget, conveniently or through theological ignorance, that the "religion" being attacked is a figment of Milton's imagination, not the religion of the Catholic Church or the Protestant churches).

Yet such a reading misses the most obvious interpretation, an interpretation that stares one in the face upon first perusal of the title page. The novel is entitled *Frankenstein; or, The Modern Prometheus*, clearly equating Victor Frankenstein with Prometheus, not with Zeus, or God. Furthermore, the epigraph from *Paradise Lost* is clearly an ironic reference to the Monster's rebuke to Frankenstein for having created him, equating the Monster with Promethean "man", not with the creation of man by God. The Monster is a "monster" because his creation was a monstrous act of disobedience and deception, a usurpation of power beyond the bounds of legitimacy. The Monster is a bastard; he is illegitimate; he lacks the brotherhood of man because he does not have the same Father as the rest of man. He is doomed by the sin of his own iniquitous father to be an outcast from "birth". It is, therefore, for this reason that he utters the complaint of Milton's Adam against his Promethean father. He might as easily have echoed the complaint of Edmund in *King Lear*, ending with Edmund's cry of self-destructive defiance: "Now, gods, stand up for bastards" (1.2.22).[4] In *King Lear*, as in *Frankenstein*, the rage of the illegitimate son reaps havoc on all and sundry, ending with the destruction of the illegitimate son himself. In both works, the father of the illegitimate child is punished for his usurpation of the natural order. Gloucester loses the eyes that had lusted after Edmund's mother; Frankenstein loses his own life and is the cause of the loss of the lives of those he loved, as (self-inflicted) punishment for the life that he brought illicitly into the world.

The impact of the monstrous imagination of Milton on the writing of *Frankenstein* is matched in importance by the "savage" ideas of Jean-Jacques Rousseau. In particular, Rousseau's *Emile* exerted a profound influence on Mary Shelley almost from infancy, through the role it played in her parents' intellectual development. William Godwin, her father, claimed that reading *Emile* had changed his life. Her mother, Mary Wollstonecraft, considered Rousseau to be the foremost authority on education, though she criticized his views on the education of women in her own work, *A Vindication of the Rights of Women*. When Percy Shelley undertook to educate his untutored lover during the early days of their relationship, he began by reading *Emile* with her; and they read it again during the period in which *Frankenstein* was being written. Its influence on the novel can be seen most lucidly in the

---

[4] *King Lear*, ed. Joseph Pearce, Ignatius Critical Editions (San Francisco: Ignatius Press, 2008). Text references are to act, scene, and line.

account of the Monster's vicarious education and also in Rousseau's attacks on the monstrous "magic" of technology. With regard to the former, the opening lines of *Emile* resonate clearly with the Monster's "education" and his conclusion that the history of man illustrates that he poisons everything in which he comes into contact. "Everything is good as it leaves the hands of the Author of things; everything degenerates in the hands of man," writes Rousseau. He continues: "[Man] mixes and confuses the climates, the elements, the seasons. He mutilates his dog, his horse, his slave. He turns everything upside down; he disfigures everything; he loves deformity, monsters. He wants nothing as nature made it, not even man."[5] Compare this with the conclusion of the Monster after he had been introduced to the history of mankind: "For a long time I could not conceive how one man could go forth to murder his fellow, or even why there were laws and governments; but when I heard details of vice and bloodshed, my wonder ceased, and I turned away with disgust and loathing."[6] Here we see the Monster, cast in the role of Rousseau's noble savage, sitting in judgment over the decadence of humanity. Yet we also see in the Monster's words an echo of Frankenstein's reaction to the Monster's "birth", especially if they are conflated with the words of Rousseau. In the making of the Monster, Frankenstein "mixes and confuses ... the elements"; he "mutilates"; he "loves deformity, monsters"; he "wants nothing as nature made it, not even man". Finally, because man "disfigures everything" and because "everything degenerates

---

[5] Jean-Jacques Rousseau, *Émile*, trans. Barbara Foxley, Introduction by P. D. Jimack (London: J. M. Dent; North Clarendon, Vt.: Tuttle Publishing, 1993), p. 5.

[6] *Frankenstein*, ed. Joseph Pearce, Ignatius Critical Editions (San Francisco: Ignatius Press, 2008), p. 123.

in the hands of man", Frankenstein looks upon his creation and, unlike God, "the Author of things", he finds that it is bad. His "wonder ceased", and he "turns away with disgust and loathing". Compare this with Mary Shelley's actual description of Frankenstein's reaction to the "birth" of his creature: "I had desired it with an ardour that far exceeded moderation; but now that I had finished, the beauty of the dream vanished, and breathless horror and disgust filled my heart."[7]

Further definitive proof of the importance of Rousseau's *Emile* as an inspirational source for *Frankenstein* can be found in Rousseau's disparaging description of the attempt of chemists to "hatch" human life in a test tube:

> Would anyone believe, if he did not have the proof, that human foolishness could have been brought to this point? Amatus Lusitanus affirmed that he had seen a little man an inch long, closed up in a bottle, whom Julius Camillus, like another Prometheus, had made by the science of alchemy. Paracelsus, *De natura rerum*, teaches the way to produce these little men and maintains that the pygmies, the fauns, the satyrs, and the nymphs were engendered by chemistry.[8]

Even if such a vision was only an unreal nightmare in Rousseau's time, it would become a nightmare reality two centuries later. Human foolishness could indeed be brought to this point—and to this point and beyond. Prometheus knows no bounds.

The connection with the noble savagery of Rousseau brands Mary Shelley as a literary luddite. Like the literal luddites who were her exact contemporaries (the luddite riots taking place from 1812 to 1818), she distrusted science

[7] Ibid., p. 49.
[8] Rousseau, *Émile*, p. 285.

and the encroachments of industrialism. She was at one with the earlier generation of Romantics, such as Blake, Coleridge, and Wordsworth, who wrote disparagingly of the "dark satanic mills" of the newly emergent industrial conurbations. This understanding of the political applicability of *Frankenstein* dominated earlier criticism of the novel, particularly in the early and mid-twentieth century when ludditism was *de rigueur* and when writers as diverse as George Orwell, T. S. Eliot, J. R. R. Tolkien, C. S. Lewis, Aldous Huxley, Evelyn Waugh, G. K. Chesterton, Hilaire Belloc, Oscar James Campbell, Siegfried Sassoon, and Edith Sitwell were railing against scientism and the ugliness of modernity. In recent years, the solid reliability of such criticism has been usurped by a generation of cynically jaundiced and jaded critics who have deconstructed meaning on the altar of idolatrous ideology and fallacious philosophy. In spite of such postmodern criticism, the traditional reading of *Frankenstein* as an indictment of unethical science prevails in the popular consciousness. An example of this was exhibited recently in the European press with the dubbing of genetically modified food as "Frankenstein Foods" or "Frankenfoods".

The final and most fascinating facet of *Frankenstein* is the extent of Percy Shelley's influence on the work, and the extent to which the novel can be read as Mary Shelley's emergence from the poet's previously pervasive shadow. Is the novel a product of Shelley's "creation" of Mary Shelley in his own image, or is it a symbol of Mary's liberation from his influence? Is Percy Shelley the real Prometheus? Is Mary the Monster? Does she resent her "creator's" power over her and the way in which he has attempted to mold her into his own image? Is she horrified by the monster she has become and the destruction she has caused? Does the novel represent a cry for help, or the first whisper of defiance against the destructive influence of her lover-mentor? These questions, if answered, may contain the key to the deepest meaning of the work.

J. Paul Hunter emphasized the extent to which Mary Shelley differed from her parents and from Percy Shelley, and how she was resentful of their influence and suspicious of some of their core beliefs:

> Readers who know well the writings of William Godwin, Mary Wollstonecraft, and Percy Shelley often notice how different *Frankenstein* is in spirit from their work, how much less trustful Mary is of creativity, the imagination, intellectual ambition, and writing itself. Her feelings towards her parents and lover—all three of them important mentors to her, and powerful intimidating presences—were decidedly mixed: her admiration of each was strong, but so was resistance and suspicion (not always conscious or articulated) of their lives, their stories, their values, their books.[9]

Taken together, the triumvirate of Godwin, Wollstonecraft, and Shelley—Mary's father, mother, and lover—represent atheism, feminism, a rejection of traditional concepts of marriage and family, and a credulous belief in inexorably beneficent "progress". As products of the superciliously self-named "Enlightenment", they espoused an early form of the secular fundamentalism that is rife today. In consequence, their beliefs, and Mary's reaction to them, retain a real relevance.

The most obvious and direct evidence of Percy Shelley's influence on the writing of *Frankenstein* is to be found in his editing of Mary's original manuscript. Although the editing was relatively minor, it discloses several significant instances of the way in which their respective philosophies

---

[9] Hunter, Preface to *Frankenstein* (Norton Critical Edition), p. ix.

differ. For example, it is evident throughout the manuscript that Mary is not an atheist but, on the contrary, that she assumes the existence of a sacred animating principle that it is perilous to usurp. This, of course, was as anathema to her atheistic lover as it was to her atheistic father. Percy undermined Mary's notion that Frankenstein's pursuit of the Monster was "a task enjoined by heaven", adding his atheistic concept of a universe determined mechanistically by "the mechanical impulse of some power of which I was unconscious".[10] Mary's pro-active "heaven"—and, logically by extension, "God"—is reduced to a powerful "mechanical impulse". Mary's concept of omniscient providence makes way, through Percy's editorial intervention, for a belief in the juggernaut of materialism.

Perhaps the most crucial and critical difference between Mary and Percy Shelley is to be discovered in their respective understanding of creativity in general and in their understanding of the role of the poet in particular. At the conclusion of "A Defense of Poetry", Percy Shelley asserts that poets are "compelled to serve the power which is seated on the throne of their own soul", and this power "is less their spirit than the spirit of the age", and that poets are "the mirrors of the gigantic shadows which futurity casts upon the present".[11] Poets, for Shelley, are slaves of the zeitgeist and servants of the future, living for today in the belief that tomorrow will be better. The future, not the past, is the root of reality, and "progress", not tradition, should be the guide to which humanity owes its allegiance. It is clear that Percy Shelley's blind faith in the power of "progress" and in the irrepressible benignity of the future sits very uncomfortably beside Mary's

---

[10] *Frankenstein*, p. 197.
[11] Shelley, "Defense of Poetry", p. 140.

luddite mistrust of scientific progress and her implicit preference for traditionalism. In her own "defense of poetry", as it emerges in the novel, the idealized or romanticized Romantic poet, as represented by the faithful Clerval, has much more in common with the tradition-oriented and profoundly Christian Romanticism of Wordsworth and Coleridge, or even with Sir Walter Scott, than with the iconoclastic "futurism" and dark egocentrism of her lover. Clerval's "favourite study consisted in books of chivalry and romance", and Frankenstein recalls nostalgically that "when very young, I can remember, that we used to act plays composed by him out of these favourite books, the principal characters of which were Orlando, Robin Hood, Amadis, and St. George".[12] Clerval, therefore, is presented as a neo-medievalist who gains his inspiration not from "the gigantic shadows which futurity casts upon the present", but from the traditional and romantic shadows of the past. Later in the novel, when Frankenstein remembers Clerval as his "beloved friend" and as "a being formed in the 'very poetry of nature'",[13] he cites lines from Wordsworth's "Tintern Abbey" as best exemplifying Clerval's serene and blessed spirit, thereby connecting Clerval, unwittingly perhaps, with Wordsworth's embryonic Christian vision. The connection with Wordsworth and Coleridge is made even more apparent when Clerval expresses his joy at being in the Lake District, the area specifically associated with Wordsworth, Coleridge, and Southey, known collectively as the "Lake Poets". "I could pass my life here," says Clerval, "and among these mountains I should scarcely regret Switzerland and the Rhine."[14]

[12] *Frankenstein*, p. 28.
[13] Ibid., p. 149.
[14] Ibid., p. 155.

Frankenstein states that "in Clerval I saw the image of my former self",[15] indicating that he had once shared the blessed serenity of Clerval's "light" Romanticism but had slipped through pride into darkness and into a darker vision of reality. Although the parallels between Frankenstein's alienation from Clerval and Percy Shelley's much-publicized rejection of Wordsworth are palpable, it is questionable that the comparison was intentional on Mary Shelley's part. Nonetheless, Clerval is, along with Elizabeth, the most unambiguously and sympathetically portrayed character in the whole novel and is, at the same time, the antithesis of Percy Shelley's ideal poet. Mary's ideal is the opposite of Shelley's and is, indeed, its antidote.

In a similar vein, Frankenstein speaks of his "pleasure in dwelling on the recollections of childhood, before misfortune had tainted my mind, and changed its bright visions of extensive usefulness into gloomy and narrow reflections upon self".[16] It is difficult to read such lines and to consider such sentiments without calling to mind Wordsworth's "Intimations of Immortality from Recollections of Early Childhood" or his immortal childlike lines from "The Rainbow":

> The Child is father of the Man;
> And I could wish my days to be
> Bound each to each by natural piety.

Mary Shelley, well versed in the Romantic poets, appears to be making the distinction between the union of wisdom and childlike innocence, encapsulated in these lines of Wordsworth, and the narrow gloominess of obsessive self-reflection as exhibited in the poetry of Byron and

[15] Ibid., p. 151.
[16] Ibid., p. 29.

Shelley. She seems, once again, to be siding with the older Romantic poets in spite of Shelley's much-publicized attacks upon them.

Perhaps the most telling evidence of Mary Shelley's sympathies with the "light" Romanticism of Wordsworth and Coleridge as opposed to the "dark" Romanticism of Byron and Shelley is in the recurring reference in *Frankenstein* to Coleridge's *The Rime of the Ancient Mariner*. At the beginning of the novel, in Captain Walton's second letter to his sister, he quotes from Coleridge's poem and states, reassuringly, that since he will "kill no albatross"[17] she need not fear for his safety. In *The Rime of the Ancient Mariner*, a profoundly Christian allegory, the killing of the albatross is symbolic of sin and the taboo attached to the sinful act, and there is a clear connection between the crime of Coleridge's Mariner and the crime of Mary Shelley's Frankenstein. In each case, the misguided protagonist ignores the taboo, taking the Promethean or satanic option and paying the consequences of so doing. This is made even more apparent when Coleridge's poem is quoted again, immediately after Frankenstein has brought the Monster to life. Frankenstein flees from the horrific vision,

> like one who, on a lonely road,
>   Doth walk in fear and dread,
> And, having once turn'd round, walks on,
>   And turns no more his head;
> Because he knows a frightful fiend
>   Doth close behind him tread.[18]

Mary's choice of these lines from Coleridge's *Rime*, at this critical juncture in the story, suggests strongly that she is

[17] Ibid., p. 16.
[18] Ibid., p. 51.

equating Frankenstein's heinous sin of bringing the Monster to life with the Mariner's heinous sin of killing the albatross. Such a suggestion is strengthened further by her description of the Monster as "demoniacal" and as "a thing such as even Dante could not have conceived".[19] It is evident that Mary is working on the level not merely of physics but of metaphysics. The Monster is not a mere product of science but is the consequence of satanic choice. It is not only monstrous, like Godzilla or King Kong, but is demonic, like Satan and his servants. Mary Shelley's work transcends the physical limitations of Percy Shelley's "gloomy and narrow" atheism and enters the infinite and eternal realm of religion, making the leap from the finite to the infinite with the chosen assistance of two of the most profoundly Christian poets, Coleridge and Dante.

If the connection with Coleridge and Dante is suggestive of the traditional morality at the heart of Mary Shelley's vision, it is made even more apparent a few pages later through the words of the character Elizabeth. "Everyone adored Elizabeth,"[20] we were told when she was first introduced, and she is depicted throughout as a sweet-hearted and gentle-spirited soul who combines an abundance of sanity and sanctity. Everyone adores Elizabeth because Mary Shelley intends that we do so. She might be seen, within the wider context of the novel, as Mary's presentation of the idealized or perfect woman, as her Beatrice or "Beatrific vision", just as Clerval is her presentation of the idealized or perfect poet, who can be seen as being akin to Dante's vision of Virgil.

The letter from Elizabeth to Victor Frankenstein, handed to Frankenstein by Clerval, contains compelling

[19] Ibid., p. 50.
[20] Ibid., p. 27.

evidence of Mary Shelley's moral vision. With adept feminine finesse and an adroitness of touch, Elizabeth seeks to draw Frankenstein away from his pride and morbidity in order to restore him to spiritual health, much as Clerval's love had restored him to physical health. Her technique (and Mary's) is to use her discussion of Ernest, Victor Frankenstein's younger brother, as a thinly veiled plea to Victor himself to change his ways. If we substitute Victor's name for Ernest's and see Elizabeth's use of the words "advocate" (lawyer) and "judge" as euphemisms for "scientist", her motives become clear:

> My uncle and I conversed a long time last night about what profession Ernest should follow. His constant illness when young has deprived him of the habits of application; and now that he enjoys good health, he is continually in the open air, climbing the hills, or rowing on the lake. I therefore proposed that he should be a farmer; which you know, Cousin, is a favourite scheme of mine. A farmer's is a very healthy happy life; and the least hurtful, or rather the most beneficial profession of any. My uncle had an idea of his being educated as an advocate, that through his interest he might become a judge. But, besides that he is not at all fitted for such an occupation, it is certainly more creditable to cultivate the earth for the sustenance of man, than to be the confidant, and sometimes the accomplice, of his vices; which is the profession of a lawyer. I said, that the employments of a prosperous farmer, if they were not a more honourable, they were at least a happier species of occupation than that of a judge, whose misfortune it was always to meddle with the dark side of human nature. My uncle smiled, and said, that I ought to be an advocate myself, which put an end to the conversation on that subject.[21]

[21] Ibid., pp. 55–56.

Elizabeth is, of course, being an advocate herself in the very letter she is writing, advocating (if we read between the lines) that Victor should give up his meddling with the dark side of human nature and pursue instead a healthier life and a more honorable occupation. It seems inescapable that Mary intends that we, the readers, should read between the lines as Elizabeth clearly intends that Victor should. Similarly, in the penultimate paragraph of Elizabeth's letter, we see how Elizabeth (and Mary) indulge "in a little gossip concerning the good people of Geneva" in order to convey another message hidden between the lines. We learn of Miss Mansfield's "approaching marriage", of how her sister "married M. Duvillard", and of the fact that Victor's "favourite schoolfellow" was "on the point of marrying".[22] The fact that all the gossip involves marriage suggests strongly that Elizabeth is dropping subtle, or not so subtle, hints that Victor should be taking the appropriate steps to marry her. One is tempted to suspect that these lines might also have been intended as a hint by Mary to her lover that he should be taking the appropriate steps "to make an honest woman of her" through marriage. Such a suspicion is strengthened by the fact that Elizabeth's letter is early in the novel and was, therefore, probably written during the summer of 1816, at which time Mary and Percy were unmarried, having had their son out of wedlock earlier in the same year. If this is so, and the fact that they were married later the same year (rather tactlessly and tastelessly within days of the discovery of Harriet Shelley's body) suggests that it is, it is evident that Mary Shelley was craving the very "conventional family values" that had been rejected by her father and lover. Even if this were not so, it is evident that Elizabeth upholds such values; and the

[22] Ibid., p. 58.

fact that she is cast in the role of a sane and saintly heroine, and later as an innocent victim, in contrast to the mad and evil actions of Frankenstein and the Monster, suggests that we are meant to sympathize with the values she espouses. The same should be said of Elizabeth's attitude to farming with its "healthy happy life", in contrast to the implied criticism of technology, of which the Monster can be said to be a metaphor. The pro-agrarian and anti-industrial stance of Elizabeth (and Mary) places her firmly in the camp of the "retrogressive" pastoral traditionalists, such as Blake or Cobbett, rather than with the "progressive" followers of futurity. Once again, Mary Shelley seems to be emerging as a veritable contradiction of many of Godwin's and Shelley's most preciously held beliefs.

The irony of Mary Shelley's most celebrated novel, an irony heightened by the plethora of feminist and postmodernist criticism that has blighted it in recent years, is that *Frankenstein* is animated by a vision very different from that which is imagined by many of its modern admirers. It is true that its author's youthful vision is darkened by her experience of Percy Shelley's arrogance and Byron's brooding, but, at its deepest levels of meaning, it is informed by, and desirous of, Coleridge's clarity and Wordsworth's wisdom. The teenage author, as the victim of the "freedoms" championed by her father and her lover (and, posthumously, by a legion of contemporary critics of her work), seems to be longing to escape into the peace and purity of traditional morality. Perhaps, indeed, there is evidence of her angst-driven longing in the words she places in the mouth of Frankenstein himself:

I enjoyed this scene; and yet my enjoyment was embittered both by the memory of the past, and the anticipation of the future. I was formed for peaceful happiness. During my youthful days discontent never visited my mind; and if I was ever overcome by *ennui*, the sight of what is beautiful in nature, or the study of what is excellent and sublime in the productions of man, could always interest my heart, and communicate elasticity to my spirits. But I am a blasted tree; the bolt has entered my soul; and I felt then that I should survive to exhibit, what I shall soon cease to be—a miserable spectacle of wrecked humanity, pitiable to others, and abhorrent to myself.[23]

In these wistful lines, a lament for lost innocence, might we see a microcosmic reiteration of the moral of the work, and the author's inspiration for writing it? Isn't there more than a suggestion that the pursuit of the illicit, the eating of the forbidden fruit, leads to lost innocence and the self-loathing that accompanies despair? Has Mary Shelley discovered that the "freedoms" offered by Godwin and Shelley, and by other tempters of humanity, are not only elusive but illusory? Has she learned the hard way that such "freedoms" do not make men into gods, or women into goddesses, but that they turn men into monsters and women into their willing victims? Isn't there more than a sneaking suspicion that *Frankenstein*, far from being a feminist work, is the vision of lost innocence screaming to be liberated from its "liberation" and longing to be free from its abuse by Promethean promiscuity?

[23] Ibid., pp. 153–54.

Chapter Seven

Wuthering Heights

Very little is known about Emily Brontë. She was born on July 30, 1818, at Thornton, near Bradford in Yorkshire, the fifth child of Patrick and Maria Brontë. She had three elder sisters—Maria, Elizabeth, and Charlotte—and one elder brother, Branwell. Her only younger sibling, Anne, was born on January 17, 1820. Shortly after Anne's birth, the family moved to Haworth, a small town on the edge of the Yorkshire moors, near Keighley, where Emily's father, an ordained minister of the Church of England, had been granted perpetual curacy. The Reverend Patrick Brontë would serve his parish devoutly and diligently for the next forty years, preaching his last sermon in October 1859, when he was eighty-two years old.

On September 15, 1821, when Emily was only three years old, her mother died. Thereafter, Emily and the other Brontë children were looked after by their aunt, Miss Elizabeth Branwell, their mother's elder sister, who took on the duties of housekeeper. In 1825, tragedy struck once again. Maria died in early May, and Elizabeth six weeks later. Thus, by the age of six, Emily had suffered the loss of her mother and two of her sisters.

The rest of Emily Brontë's life was largely uneventful. She never left her home in Haworth, except for a handful of short periods, all of which were for a few months only.

Except for six months at school in Lancashire, when she was six years old, and nine months in Brussels in 1842, she seems to have rarely journeyed beyond a few miles of Haworth. She never married and appears never to have had a serious love affair. Apart from her novel, and a handful of essays and poems, she wrote very little of lasting value.

These are the bare facts, the bare bones of her life. She seems to have been a home-loving daughter of a clergyman who lived chastely until the end of her days. There is little else to know and, one would have thought, little else to say. Gossips, however, do not need facts and, shame to say, many modern biographers and many literary academics seem to be little than gossips. In a shameful and shameless display of myth making, these "scholars" have taken the bare bones of Emily Brontë's life and have transformed them into skeletons ensconced in a closet of their own devising. Thus, the virginal clergyman's daughter has been turned into a fulminating feminist, a militant Marxist, a homosexual, an avowed atheist, a pantheist, an anti-Christian polemicist, and a courageous heretic. In the hands of these latter-day Victor Frankensteins, a monstrous Emily Brontë has been created. Taking away her virginity (posthumously!) and exorcising her Christianity, which in the modern academy is the love that dare not speak its name, she is made to come out of the imaginary closet. Of course, and needless to say, the real Emily Brontë does not emerge from such a closet, not least because the closet contains nothing but the "emperor's new clothes". (How different are these closed-minded closets from the open-hearted wisdom to be found in C. S. Lewis' Wardrobe!)

Charles Simpson, in his 1929 biography of Emily Brontë, which was described by Lucasta Miller in *The Brontë Myth* as "the sanest life of Emily to appear in a period otherwise dominated by lurid legend-mongering", speculated about what these legend-mongers would feel "if they could for a moment see Emily in the flesh and compare her with the figure of their imaginations.... Seldom has a phantom so vast and so shadowy been raised above a personality so elusive."[1] Since we do not have Emily's real presence to vanquish the monstrous phantoms, we will have to rely on solid scholarship to do so in her absence. In this regard, there is no better place to start than with Miller's *Brontë Myth*. With devastatingly incisive precision, she dissects the woeful errors in Brontë studies over the past century, destroying the credibility of much that passes for "scholarship". Her work is so impressive that all serious and conscientious scholars of the Brontës could do worse than to commence their studies by reading this masterful critique of their less-than-conscientious forebears.

Having exposed the naked shame of the emperors (and empresses) who have attempted to make of Emily Brontë a monster created in their own image, we are left with the naked truth that the author of *Wuthering Heights* was a home-loving Victorian woman who was completely content living in the parsonage with her father, a faithful Christian minister. Furthermore, since there is absolutely no evidence to the contrary, we must assume that she lived chastely until the end of her days. As the virgin daughter of a country parson, Emily Brontë's life is simply too dull to be tolerated by those seeking scandal. It is, therefore, unsurprising that the lurid-minded have sought to spice up her homespun life with a little illicit (and fictional) spice! A lie is, however, a lie, however artfully constructed (or deconstructed).

[1] Lucasta Miller, *The Brontë Myth* (New York: Anchor Books, 2005), p. 222.

Having established the seemingly unavoidable fact that Emily Brontë was a soberly conventional Victorian lady, we find ourselves confronted with the darkness and passion of her novel. How can one seemingly so innocuous create something seemingly so monstrous? How can an apparently prim and proper parson's daughter have created a Heathcliff and a Catherine? It is this apparent anomaly that has sparked much of the debate as to the true beliefs of Emily Brontë. Critics of her novel have read, or more often misread, its meaning and have projected the perceived meaning into the mind and personality of its author. Feminists have detected a feminist meaning to the novel and have concluded, therefore, that Emily was a feminist; Marxists have detected a socialist message in the novel and have proclaimed, thereby, that Emily was a revolutionary; anti-Christians have discovered attacks on conventional Christianity—so they believe—and have lauded Emily as a heretic or an atheist. In each case, the critic has approached the text with prejudiced preconceptions and has found his own prejudices reflected back at him; then, having created the meaning of the book in his own image, he makes Emily in his own image also. Such criticism is merely a mirror of the critic's own prejudices, reflecting only what he wants to see. The mirror is, in fact, a mire of narcissistic self-deception.

In order to get beyond this flawed approach to literature, we need to forsake the mirror and seek instead a lens that will enable us to focus objectively on the novel's true meaning. Almost invariably, the best lens for focusing on a novel, or a poem, or any work of literature is the eye of the author. We need to see *Wuthering Heights* through Emily's eyes if we wish to see it and understand it as she did. Once we succeed in doing this, we will see *Wuthering*

Heights without the withering depths of inanity that pass as criticism of the novel. Furthermore, if we succeed in looking at the novel through Emily Brontë's eyes, we will have the added pleasure of getting to know her better, not as we or others would wish her to be, but as she is. We will get to know the real flesh-and-blood woman who was Emily Brontë and not the mere myth she has become.

In order to approach *Wuthering Heights* through Emily Brontë's eyes, we have to begin with Emily Brontë herself, not with any figment of our own imagination; we have to begin with the tangible and objectively verifiable evidence of her life. In short, we have to begin with the known facts, as already presented—which is to say that we need to begin with a chaste and home-loving parson's daughter in early Victorian England. If we do this, we should expect to see evidence of a Christian moral perspective and would be surprised if it were absent. If, on the other hand, we fail to approach the text through the eyes of the author, we might fail to see the evidence even if it stares us in the face. Take, for instance, Stevie Davies, in her book *Emily Brontë: Heretic*.[2] Quoting from Emily Brontë's essay "The Butterfly", in which Emily wrote that "the entire creation is equally meaningless ... the universe seemed to me a vast machine constructed solely to produce evil", Davies concludes that Emily was a "heretic" who denied the possibility of a benevolent God and a benign natural order.[3] Certainly, Emily's words, as quoted, would suggest that Davies is right and that the seemingly gentle parson's daughter had rejected everything her father believed. If these are her beliefs, she is

[2] Stevie Davies, *Emily Brontë: Heretic* (London: Women's Press, 1994).
[3] "The Butterfly by Emily J. Brontë: August 11th 1842", in *The Belgian Essays: Charlotte Brontë and Emily Brontë* (London: Yale University Press, 1997).

indeed a heretic. Yet the citation, taken in isolation, is woefully misleading. "The Butterfly" portrays Nature unflinchingly as being destructively cruel, yet Emily's purpose is to contrast the "cruelty" of Nature with the love of God. The Butterfly appears amid the natural chaos of the Forest "like a censuring angel sent from heaven", its "large wings of gleaming gold and purple ... a symbol of the world to come—just as the ugly caterpillar is the beginning of the splendid butterfly, this globe is the embryo of a new heaven and a new earth whose meagrest beauty infinitely surpasses mortal imagination."[4] Are these the words of a heretic who denies the possibility of a benevolent God? Clearly not; they are more like the words of a parson's daughter. And lest we still doubt her deepest meaning, her theological conclusion, or her overarching moral, she removes any lingering doubts with the proclamation that "God is the God of justice and mercy"[5] and that suffering is but the seed for a divine harvest. Here we see not only the parson's daughter, but the parson's daughter proclaiming the Gospel from the hilltops. Those who expect to see the parson's daughter will not be surprised; those who, blinded by their own prejudice, refuse to see the parson's daughter will ignore the truth even when it makes itself as plain as day. There are none so blind as those who will not see.

Similarly, Emily's famous poem that commences with the line "No coward soul is mine" is often cited as evidence of her feminism or her "free spirit" or her rebellious nature. Yet her soul is not cowardly not because it is a "free spirit" that spurns the patriarchal society but because it resides in the love of God:

[4] Ibid., p. 47.
[5] Ibid.

No coward soul is mine,
No trembler in the world's storm-troubled sphere:
I see Heaven's glories shine,
And faith shines equal, arming me from fear.

O God within my breast,
Almighty, ever-present Deity!
Life—that in me has rest,
As I—undying Life—have power in Thee!
. . . .
With wide-embracing love
Thy spirit animates eternal years,
Pervades and broods above,
Changes, sustains, dissolves, creates and rears.

Though earth and moon were gone,
And suns and universes ceased to be,
And Thou were left alone,
Every existence would exist in Thee.

There is not room for Death,
Nor atom that his might could render void:
Thou—THOU art Being and Breath,
And what THOU art may never be destroyed.

Are these the words of a feminist heretic in rebellion against a patriarchal society? Hardly. On the contrary, one suspects that the Reverend Patrick Brontë would have been proud of his daughter's words of courageous faith.

A misreading of the text is possible even among more diligent scholars. Lucasta Miller goes astray when she seeks to make a distinction between Charlotte Brontë's vision of heaven and Emily's:

In contrast, in *Wuthering Heights*, Emily had presented heaven as a far less welcoming prospect. When Cathy dreams that she has been there, it is a place of exile, not rapture: "[H]eaven did not seem to be my home," she tells Nelly, "and I broke my heart with weeping to come back to earth; and the angels were so angry that they flung me out, into the middle of the heath on top of Wuthering Heights; where I woke sobbing for joy."[6]

Pace Miller, Emily does not present heaven "as a far less welcoming prospect" than does her sister, Charlotte; she presents heaven as a less-than-welcoming prospect for Catherine, a character in the novel. It is not an unwelcome prospect for Emily, as the poem above makes clear, nor is it an unwelcome prospect for the perennially wise Nelly, to whom Catherine is speaking. It is unwelcome for Catherine, not because heaven is unwelcoming, but because Catherine does not welcome it. The angels merely give her what she wants. Such a view of heaven, and the unrepentant sinner's alienation from it, is profoundly orthodox. It can be seen in the teaching of St. Thomas Aquinas and is described in Dante's *Divine Comedy* and, more recently, in C. S. Lewis' *The Great Divorce*.

The connection between Dante, Lewis, and Emily Brontë is not as surprising as we might at first suppose. Let's look a little closer at what they have in common and how they differ. *The Divine Comedy* presents us with a vision of heaven, purgatory, and hell, "the vision of perfection, the vision of improvement, and the vision of failure",[7] as G. K. Chesterton so memorably put it; *The Great Divorce* presents us with a vision of the twilight zone between hell and purgatory, with heaven as a powerful presence offstage; and *Wuthering Heights* presents us with hell alone, but with purgatory and heaven powerfully

[6] Miller, *Brontë Myth*, p. 197.
[7] G. K. Chesterton, *Heretics* (New York: John Lane Company, 1909), p. 30.

(and paradoxically) present in their (apparent) absence. This paradoxical presence of purgatory and heaven in the very midst of the hell that Emily Brontë presents to us is not, perhaps, obvious but is nonetheless axiomatic to an understanding of the underlying Christianity that permeates the deepest levels of meaning in the work. This will become increasingly obvious as we engage the text of the novel more closely.

At the deepest theological level, we can see parallels between *Wuthering Heights* and Emily's essay "The Butterfly". In both works, we are confronted, uncomfortably, with unflinching cruelty, which, in the apparent absence of a benevolent God, seems to be "meaningless" so that "the universe seemed to me a vast machine constructed solely to produce evil".[8] As we have seen, the "natural" chaos and cruelty of the Forest, as depicted in the essay, is redeemed by the arrival of the Butterfly, "like a censuring angel sent from heaven", its "large wings of gleaming gold and purple ... a symbol of the world to come ... of a new heaven and a new earth whose meagrest beauty infinitely surpasses mortal imagination." The considerable extent of Emily's grasp of Christian symbolism is evident in her choice of gold and purple for the Butterfly's wings: gold representing the glory of God, and purple the sins of humanity. It is only through penance (purple) that we can inherit the glory (gold) of the new heaven and new earth, and the Butterfly, as "a censuring angel sent from heaven", is vested in such a way as to remind us of this sobering fact.

If Emily was well versed in Christian symbolism, she would also, no doubt, have been conversant with the symbolism employed by the Romantic poets that she so evidently admired. It is, therefore, intriguing that one of

---

[8] Brontë, "The Butterfly", *Belgian Essays*.

the couplets in William Blake's "Auguries of Innocence" seems ideally suited to serve as an epigraph for "The Butterfly", so much so that one is tempted to suggest that it was this particular couplet that had served as Emily's initial inspiration:

> Kill not the Moth nor Butterfly,
> For the Last Judgment draweth nigh.

As with Emily's overarching moral in her essay, Blake condemns wanton cruelty and couples it with an eschatological omen. Another couplet in the same poem is suggestive of the emergent moral in *Wuthering Heights*:

> The Lamb misus'd breeds Public strife
> And yet forgives the Butcher's Knife.

In *Wuthering Heights*, the abusing of the Lamb does indeed breed public strife, the Lamb being a recurrent image in Blake's poetry signifying both innocence and Christ. But what of the significance of the second half of the couplet? Surely, there is little evidence in *Wuthering Heights* of any forgiveness of the "butchers" on the part of those abused by them. Isn't there, instead, a seemingly endless cycle of bitter and futile revenge? Yes, there is, but this doesn't contradict Blake's couplet.

Let's read it again more carefully. If the Lamb signifies Christ, we can see that Christ does indeed forgive the butcher's knife—and, if he repents, even the butcher himself! So far so good. But what of the Lamb as a symbol of innocence, or the innocent? Do the innocent forgive the butcher's knife? Can the innocent forgive cruelty? Can the innocent forgive those who have destroyed their innocence? From a Christian perspective, and let's not forget that Blake and Brontë had a Christian perspective, the answer is yes—but only if the innocent retain or regain their innocence. A Christian is called upon by Christ to love his enemy, not merely his neighbor.

What, one might pertinently ask, has all this to do with *Wuthering Heights*? The "public strife" running rampant through the length and breadth of the novel is caused not only by the cruelty inflicted by "the butcher's knife" but by the lack of forgiveness and the desire for revenge. The innocent do not forgive the butcher's knife but become butchers themselves, destroying the innocence of others. The result is a destructive chain reaction in which more and more innocent lambs are turned into vengeful wolves. This is the very animus of the novel and the impetus of its plot. The absence of the Lamb's forgiveness is the very root of the evil that afflicts the characters of the novel. Thus, paradoxically, the Lamb's absence is the invisible presence that animates the action of the whole work.

Emily's employment of such Christian imagery is not merely a curious digression, on her part or mine, but, on the contrary, it offers us the means to understanding *Wuthering Heights*. Just as the butterfly in the essay is a symbol that "God is the God of justice and mercy", so the essay itself can be seen as a symbol of—or more correctly a metaphor for—the novel. As a metaphor of *Wuthering Heights*, "The Butterfly" also serves as the key to unlock it. Put simply and bluntly, the critic needs to forget about the red herrings of perverse conjecture and pursue instead the elusive butterfly of Christian symbolism that flutters, often unnoticed, through the pages of Emily Brontë's work.

If we see such symbolism in her essay, we should expect to find it in her novel. For the most part, the Christianity of the novel is seen in the words and actions of Nelly Dean. She is the Butterfly, "the censuring angel", manifesting "the God of justice and mercy", who attempts to bring the plot's protagonists to their senses.

In volume 1, chapter 7, Nelly reprimands Heathcliff for grieving Catherine, warning him, in words that serve both as prophecy and as a moral for the whole book, that "proud people breed sad sorrows for themselves."[9] One wonders whether Heathcliff carries these words with him as the story unfolds, whether indeed he carries them with him to the grave. Either way, it is clear that Emily Brontë intends that we, the readers, take them with us as the plot unravels before us. The whole story is the weaving of the sad sorrows brought upon the main protagonists by their own pride.

In volume 1, chapter 9, in her dialogue with Catherine concerning Edgar Linton's marriage proposal, Nelly reveals herself as the purveyor of wit and wisdom. This dialogue is so central to understanding the whole work that it warrants citation at length:

> "To-day, Edgar Linton has asked me to marry him, and I've given him an answer—Now, before I tell you whether it was a consent, or denial—you tell me which it ought to have been."
>
> "Really, Miss Catherine, how can I know?" I replied. "To be sure, considering the exhibition you performed in his presence this afternoon, I might say it would be wise to refuse him—since he asked you after that, he must either be hopelessly stupid, or a venturesome fool."[10]

Catherine informs Nelly that she had accepted his proposal and is impatient to know whether Nelly thinks she was right to have done so. "There are many things to be

[9] *Wuthering Heights*, ed. Joseph Pearce, Ignatius Critical Editions (San Francisco: Ignatius Press, 2008), p. 89.

[10] Ibid.

considered before that question can be answered properly," Nelly responds. "First and foremost, do you love Mr. Edgar?" After Catherine answers in the affirmative, Nelly puts her "through the following catechism", adding that "for a girl of twenty-two it was not injudicious". The "catechism" is so delightful and judicious that it is possibly the highlight of the whole book:

> "Why do you love him, Miss Cathy?"
> "Nonsense, I do—that's sufficient."
> "By no means; you must say why?"
> "Well, because he is handsome, and pleasant to be with."
> "Bad," was my commentary.
> "And because he is young and cheerful."
> "Bad, still."
> "And, because he loves me."
> "Indifferent, coming there."
> "And he will be rich, and I shall like to be the greatest woman of the neighbourhood, and I shall be proud of having such a husband."
> "Worst of all! And now, say how you love him?"
> "As every body loves—You're silly, Nelly."
> "Not at all—Answer."[11]

Catherine, complaining that Nelly is jesting with her, scowls and turns her face to the fire. Nelly, insisting that she is "very far from jesting", continues:

> "you love Mr. Edgar, because he is handsome, and young, and cheerful, and rich, and loves you. The last, however, goes for nothing—You would love him without that, probably; and with it you wouldn't, unless he possessed the four former attractions."

[11] Ibid., pp. 89–90.

"No, to be sure not—I should only pity him—hate him, perhaps, if he were ugly, and a clown."

"But there are several other handsome, rich young men in the world; handsomer, possibly, and richer than he is— What should hinder you from loving them?"

"If there be any, they are out of my way—I've seen none like Edgar."

"You may see some; and he won't always be handsome, and young, and may not always be rich."

"He is now; and I have only to do with the present—I wish you would speak rationally."

"Well, that settles it—if you have only to do with the present, marry Mr. Linton."[12]

The words of Nelly in this dialogue are so sagacious, and the replies of Catherine so banal, that it is impossible to avoid the conclusion that Nelly is expressing the wisdom of the author. Nelly's words are Emily's. Through this succinct catechetical exchange, we learn that Edgar is a fool for marrying Catherine and will come to regret it; we learn that Catherine's being "proud of having such a husband" was the worst answer of all, reminding us insistently of Nelly's earlier admonishment of Heathcliff that "proud people breed sad sorrows for themselves". We learn finally, at least implicitly, that those who think only of themselves, and of pursuing the passions of the present moment, are doomed to regret the folly of their imprudent impudence.

The wisdom of Nelly's words, and the suspicion that they are the words of the author speaking vicariously, are reinforced a few pages later in a further exchange between Catherine and Nelly. In this case, Nelly emerges as an incisive Christian theologian:

[12] Ibid., pp. 90–91.

"If I were in heaven, Nelly, I should be extremely miserable."

"Because you are not fit to go there," I answered. "All sinners would be miserable in heaven."[13]

Nelly's axiomatic riposte should be borne in mind as the dialogue continues, particularly in the light, or darkness, of Catherine's obsession with Heathcliff:

> My great miseries in this world have been Heathcliff's miseries, and I watched and felt each from the beginning; my great thought in living is himself. If all perished, and *he* remained, I should still continue to be; and, if all else remained, and he were annihilated, the Universe would turn to a mighty stranger. I should not seem a part of it. My love for Linton is like the foliage in the woods. Time will change it, I'm well aware, as winter changes the trees—my love for Heathcliff resembles the eternal rocks beneath—a source of little visible delight, but necessary. Nelly, I *am* Heathcliff—he's always, always in my mind—not as a pleasure, any more than I am always a pleasure to myself—but, as my own being—so, don't talk of our separation again.[14]

In this well-known passage, probably the most quoted and least understood passage in the whole work, Catherine is confessing the infernal nature of her "love" for Heathcliff. Heathcliff is not merely an idol but is Catherine's god, and not just her god but her demon also. She not only worships him, but she is possessed by him. This demonic dimension was not lost on G. K. Chesterton, who wrote that Heathcliff "fails as a man as catastrophically as he succeeds as a demon".[15] The demonic is further suggested

---

[13] Ibid., p. 92.

[14] Ibid., pp. 94–95.

[15] G. K. Chesterton, *The Victorian Age in Literature* (London: Williams & Norgate, 1913), p. 113.

by the fact that Catherine's words, "I *am* Heathcliff", echo those of Milton's Satan, "myself am hell".[16] Like Satan she is exiled from heaven because everywhere, even heaven, would be "a mighty stranger" to her if Heathcliff were not there; she would "not seem a part of it". She would rather be with him in hell than without him in heaven. Nothing will separate her from the "love" of her god, not even the love of God. She will be with Heathcliff forever, not merely "till death do us part" but beyond death itself. Heathcliff is the "eternal rock" upon which she builds her church. He is "a source of little visible delight" but, on the contrary, is "darkness visible", like Milton's Satan,[17] and the source of all her suffering. Yet she will not be separated from the hell she has chosen. She gets what she chooses. The angels in her dream merely give her what she desires. Again, and to reiterate, this is profoundly orthodox Christian theology, in the finest tradition of Dante's *Inferno*.

As for Heathcliff, we can dismiss the theory that he was modeled to any great degree on Branwell Brontë, Emily's drunk and dissolute brother. Although the pathetically weak character of Hindley Earnshaw is clearly inspired by the tragic figure of Branwell, the psychopathically strong Heathcliff is drawn from no real-life character known to Emily. He is the disfigured figment of Emily's luridly vivid imagination, inspired in all probability by the disfigured figment of another female novelist's lurid imagination. Emily Brontë's monster is probably the imaginative offspring of Mary Shelley's Monster in her most famous novel, *Frankenstein*, published in the year that Emily was born. Heathcliff reaps havoc and destruction, but, as with Mary Shelley's creature, he is also "demoniacal".[18] He is

---

[16] John Milton, *Paradise Lost*, bk. 4, line 75.

[17] Ibid., bk. 1, line 63.

[18] See Mary Shelley, *Frankenstein*, ed. Joseph Pearce, Ignatius Critical Editions (San Francisco: Ignatius Press, 2008), vol. 1, chap. 4.

physically monstrous and spiritually demonic at one and the same time, a devil incarnate. The parallels between Emily Brontë's monster-demon and Mary Shelley's "demoniacal" creature are significant and show a certain kinship of spirit between the two novelists. Whereas Mary Shelley seems to be *groping* toward traditional Christian morality *in spite* of her anti-Christian upbringing, Emily Brontë can be seen to be *grasping* the same morality *because* of her upbringing. One is in the dark groping for the light, while the other is in the light but showing us what it's like to be in the dark. If there is one significant difference in their respective approaches, it springs from the influence of Milton's heterodox musings on Shelley, and the confusion it causes to her moral vision, as opposed to the evident influence of Dante's profoundly orthodox Muse on the work of Emily, and the clarity that springs from it.

The towering influence of Dante is once more evident in the scene between Heathcliff and Catherine when the latter is on her deathbed. Catherine's "love" for Heathcliff is so disordered that it seems indistinguishable from hate. "I shall not pity you, not I," she says. "You have killed me—and thriven on it, I think."[19] The moment of death, for Heathcliff and for Catherine, is not a time for reconciliation, either with God or with each other. It is a time for bitter reproach, a time for venting one's spleen in one final act of self-destructive abandonment. "I wish I could hold you till we were both dead!" Catherine exclaims. "I shouldn't care what you suffered. I care nothing for your sufferings. Why shouldn't you suffer? I do!" Nelly, as the sole witness to the scene, places the vindictive exchange within a theological context by reminding us of Catherine's "heavenly" nightmare that had prompted

[19] *Wuthering Heights*, p. 178.

Catherine to remark that she would be "extremely miserable" in heaven:

> The two, to a cool spectator, made a strange and fearful picture. Well might Catherine deem that Heaven would be a land of exile to her, unless, with her mortal body, she cast away her mortal character also. Her present countenance had a wild vindictiveness in its white cheek, and a bloodless lip, and scintillating eye.[20]

Catherine still has no desire for heaven, preferring the hell of Heathcliff. She makes her choice and is self-condemned by it. Heathcliff, for his part, spits his venom at Catherine but would prefer to writhe with her in the Inferno, in an eternal love-hate embrace, than live without her in heaven or on earth:

> "Are you *possessed with a devil*," he pursued, savagely, "to talk in that manner to me, when you are dying? Do you reflect that all those words will be branded in my memory, and *eating deeper eternally*, after you have left me? You know you lie to say I have killed you; and, Catherine, you know that I could as soon forget you, as my existence! Is it not sufficient for your *infernal selfishness*, that while you are at peace *I shall writhe in the torments of hell?*"
> "*I shall not be at peace*," moaned Catherine.[21]

The emphasis has been added to highlight the metaphysical drama that lurks beneath the physical surface of their exchange. For Emily, as for her great forebear and inspiration, Dante, every act in life has eternal significance.

As usual, it is Nelly who is the author's voice when the moral dimension is at its most forthright. Following

[20] Ibid., p. 178.
[21] Ibid., p. 179 (italics added).

Catherine's death, Nelly tells Heathcliff that she hopes that she has gone to heaven, "where we may, everyone, join her, if we take due warning, and leave our evil ways to follow good!" Although Heathcliff appears deaf to her sermon, and in spite of all he has done, she is filled with pity for him:

> "Poor wretch!" I thought; "you have a heart and nerves the same as your brother men! Why should you be so anxious to conceal them? Your pride cannot blind God! You tempt Him to wring them, till He forces a cry of humiliation!"[22]

In her efforts to comfort Heathcliff in his grief, she tells him that Catherine had died "quietly as a lamb": "Her life closed in a gentle dream—may she wake as kindly in the other world!" Heathcliff's response is satanic in its savagery:

> "May she wake in torment!" he cried, with frightful vehemence, stamping his foot, and groaning in a sudden paroxysm of ungovernable passion. "Why, she's a liar to the end! Where is she? Not *there*—not in heaven—not perished—where? Oh! You said you cared nothing for my sufferings! And I pray one prayer—I repeat it till my tongue stiffens—Catherine Earnshaw, may you not rest, as long as I am living! You said I killed you—haunt me, then! The murdered *do* haunt their murderers. I believe—I know that ghosts *have* wandered on the earth. Be with me always—take any form—drive me mad! only *do* not leave me in this abyss, where I cannot find you! Oh, God! it is unutterable! I *cannot* live without my life! I *cannot* live without my soul!"

---

[22] Ibid., p. 186.

He dashed his head against the knotted trunk; and, lift-
ing up his eyes, howled, not like a man, but like a savage
beast getting goaded to death with knives and spears.

I observed several splashes of blood about the bark of
the tree, and his hand and forehead were both stained.[23]

Here we see Nelly's thoughts become reality before our
eyes. Heathcliff, the "poor wretch", has tempted God "till
He forces a cry of humiliation". The sinner's hate-filled
anger reduces him to the level of a howling beast, to the
level of a man possessed by demons who strikes his own
head against a tree. The symbolism is that of an infernal
Passion: the blood-stained Tree, the scourging with knives
and spears, the bloody forehead and hand. The sinner condemns himself to self-inflicted suffering and also, at the
same time, condemns Christ to the sin-inflicted suffering
of the Cross, where He dies for the sins of the world. The
sinner's rejection of the Cross is a rejection of the mercy
of God and an acceptance, therefore, of the suffering
demanded by justice in recompense for the suffering caused
by sin. The sinner gets his just deserts not merely because
he deserves it but because he desires it. Thus, Heathcliff's
infernal prayer that another soul should "wake in torment"
is followed by a prayer that Catherine's ghost should haunt
him for the rest of his days. "Be with me always—take any
form—drive me mad!" The prayer is answered and the rest
of the novel, from Heathcliff's perspective, is the story of
his being possessed by the demon of Catherine's invisible
presence until it drives him mad. Earlier he had boasted to
the dying Catherine that "nothing that God or Satan could
inflict would have parted us, *you*, of your own will, did
it."[24] From a Christian perspective, this is profoundly true,

[23] Ibid., p. 187.
[24] Ibid., p. 181.

demonstrating once again the profundity of Emily's grasp of orthodox doctrine. God offers grace, but He will not force us to respond to its promptings; He respects our free will as the greatest gift that He has given us; if we insist on going to hell, He will not prevent us. Satan tempts us, but he cannot make us sin; our free will is beyond his grasp; he can make us slaves only if we will it. Emily Brontë leaves us with no option but to see Heathcliff as the architect of his own despair.

In the midst of the hellish brutality of Heathcliff, the raw-nerved passion of the plot, and the unremitting darkness of the atmosphere, it is easy to overlook those rare moments of feather-light subtlety in which Emily Brontë alights upon the text with the softness and beauty of a butterfly. Take, for instance, the clear allusion to the inscription above the entrance to Dante's hell ("Abandon Hope, all ye who enter here") in the following passage:

> I heard Cathy inquiring of her unsociable attendant, what was that inscription over the door?
>
> Hareton stared up, and scratched his head like a true clown.
>
> "It's some damnable writing," he answered. "I cannot read it."
>
> "Can't read it?" cried Catherine, "I can read it ... It's English ... but I want to know why it is there."[25]

From a literary perspective, we also "want to know why it is there". It serves no purpose to the unfolding of the plot except to raise the issue of Hareton's illiteracy, which could have been achieved in a much less contrived way. It seems that Emily is expecting her readers to employ their

[25] Ibid., p. 240.

literary imagination to detect her allusion to the words of the most famous inscription written over a door in the history of literature. In forcing us to make this association, she successfully equates *Wuthering Heights* with Dante's *Inferno* without bludgeoning us with overt allegory. As a literary sleight of hand, it is worthy of Shakespeare, the undoubted master of such trickery.

At this juncture, it might be prudent to address the negative characterization of Joseph, the principal "Christian" voice in the novel. Might it not be argued that such a negative portrayal of the Christian moralizer suggests an antagonism on the author's part toward Christian morality? It seems a reasonable-enough argument, but only if one stays on the superficial level where Joseph belongs. He is a superficial Christian. He is not the real thing. His lack of charity disqualifies him. Given Emily Brontë's family background and her upbringing, she obviously knew her Bible. She would certainly have known the famous passage in 1 Corinthians about love being the greatest of virtues, that those who "have not love" are nothing but "a noisy gong or a clanging cymbal" and that those who "have all faith, so as to remove mountains, but have not love" are "nothing" (13:1–2; RSV-2CE). Joseph is "nothing"; at least he is nothing like a true Christian, and Emily Brontë is merely showing a healthy Christian disdain for the puritan and the Pharisee. She is echoing Christ's condemnation of the scribe, the Pharisee, and the hypocrite. She is also following in a noble tradition of Christian literature in which the very greatest authors have sought to highlight the truth of the Gospel through exposing the hypocrisy of unfaithful or hypocritical Christians. Dante has a whole section (*bowge*) of the eighth circle of hell reserved especially for the hypocrites, and Chaucer spends much of his General Prologue exposing the hypocrisy of many of his pilgrims.

Yet Dante never lets us lose sight of heaven, showing us the shining example of Beatrice, and Chaucer gives us the example of the "povre Persoun of a toun" as an example of the "good man ... of religioun"—the perfect priest—and the example of the Plowman, the parson's brother, as an example of the perfect layman. Emily Brontë does the same as her illustrious forebears. She gives us Joseph, the hypocrite, to show us how not to be a Christian, but she also gives us Nelly Dean as the shining example of Christian sanity in the midst of the madness. The Christianity of *Wuthering Heights* emerges not through the harsh words of Joseph but through the loving words and actions of Nelly. The author's Christianity also emerges, on a transcendent metadynamic level, through the novel itself, taken as a whole, as an integrated work of literary art.

The novel ends on a light note. The darkness lifts and the emergent light lightens the burden of evil that has loomed, doom-laden, over the whole work. As Mr. Lockwood returns to Wuthering Heights, we are almost dazzled by light and lightheartedness. Love is in the air—true love, not its infernal inversion. Catherine Linton, with a voice "as sweet as a silver bell",[26] is teaching Hareton to read. Hareton's handsome features glow with pleasure as he is reproached gently for his mistakes. Afterward, he is rewarded for his efforts with "at least five kisses, which ... he generously returned". Mr. Lockwood leaves this blissful scene and makes his way to the kitchen, where he sees Nelly Dean, "sewing and singing a song". *Can this really be Wuthering Heights?* we ask ourselves. *Can this be the place that we have become accustomed to see as a living hell?* Wuthering Heights it assuredly is, but it is clearly no longer hell. It is no longer hell because the demon has departed. Heathcliff

[26] Ibid., p. 330.

is dead. When we are told as much a page or so later, we had guessed already. Happiness of this sort was not possible in his presence. It is the removal of the evil that has allowed the good to flourish. Wuthering Heights is free of its malevolent master. His death was an exorcism.

The only person who is still not happy is the puritanical Joseph, who rebukes Nelly for her singing. As judgmental as ever, he calls upon the Lord to judge those who indulge in singing and dancing, giving "glories tuh Sattan". Nelly's riposte is to tell him to be quiet and read his Bible "like a Christian", implying that his uncharitable method of reading the Scriptures is anything but Christian. In this final juxtaposition of the saintly Nelly with the sanctimonious Joseph, we see the clearest indication yet of Emily Brontë's sympathy with the true Christianity of the former and her condemnation of the Pharisaism of the latter.

The only element of ambiguity at the novel's conclusion is the doubt about the eternal destiny of Catherine Earnshaw and Heathcliff. Emily Brontë, unlike Joseph, is not prepared to sit in judgment, mindful of the words of Christ that we "judge not, lest we be judged" (see Matthew 7:1). Are the two Promethean protagonists resting in peace, or are they condemned to wander the earth as restless spirits? Have they been forgiven for their sins, or are their sins being washed away in the fires of purgatory? Or, perhaps, are they united in death, as they were in life, by their hellish passion, condemned to wander the moors for eternity, blown by the winds of disordered "love" like Dante's Paolo and Francesca? We do not know for certain because Emily Brontë doesn't tell us. We do know, however, that Catherine Linton and Hareton are to be married on New Year's Day, the symbolism of which speaks for itself, and that their love has conquered the evil legacy of their forebears: "*They* are afraid of nothing," says Lockwood, as he leaves Wuthering Heights for the last time. "Together they would brave Satan and all his legions."[27]

Even if Emily Brontë, as a good Christian, is unprepared to second-guess the Final Judgment that awaits her fictional characters, presuming not to presume such things, her happy ending serves as the final judgment on her work. The novel's conclusion illustrates quite clearly that Emily Brontë, like Catherine Linton and Hareton, and like the indomitable Nelly Dean, is on the side of the angels.

[27] Ibid., p. 362.

Chapter Eight

A Christmas Carol

It could be argued and has been argued that, after Shakespeare, Charles Dickens is the finest writer in the English language. His works have forged their way into the canon to such a degree that it is much more difficult to know which of his novels to leave off the recommended reading list than it is to choose which to include. Each of us has his favorites, and each invariably begs to differ with his neighbor's choice. True, in terms of pure brute statistics, we would be forced to concede that *A Tale of Two Cities* is most people's favorite because it is usually listed as the bestselling novel of all time, with sales exceeding two hundred million (though *Don Quixote*, which is excluded from official statistics and has never been out of print since its first publication over four hundred years ago, has probably sold more copies).

Those who are justifiably skeptical of the claim that the bestselling is necessarily the best might point to a poll conducted by the Folio Society, a de facto private members club for bibliophiles, as a more objective way of judging the best of Dickens as opposed to the most popular. More than ten thousand members of the Society voted in 1998 for their favorite books from any age. *The Lord of the Rings* triumphed; *Pride and Prejudice* was runner-up; and *David Copperfield* was third. Why, one wonders, was this particular Dickens classic selected ahead of *Nicholas Nickleby*, *Oliver Twist*, *Great Expectations*, or *Bleak House*? Who can possibly know? It's a mystery as insoluble as that surrounding Edwin Drood in Dickens' last, unfinished work. In any case, and irrespective of these populist and elitist judgments, none of these Dickensian heavyweights wins my vote as Dickens' greatest work. That accolade belongs, *me judice*, to the diminutive genius of *A Christmas Carol*.

Originally published in 1843, *A Christmas Carol* is sandwiched chronologically between *Barnaby Rudge* and *Martin Chuzzlewit*, much weightier tomes. Yet Dickens' ghost story not only punches beyond its weight but outpunches its heavyweight rivals. Switching metaphors, the character of Ebenezer Scrooge, like a genie released or unleashed from a bottle, escapes from the pages of the book to charm the collective psyche of the culture. He is a literary colossus who, without the benefit of eponymous billing, has emerged from Dickens' imaginary menagerie as a cautionary icon of mean-spirited worldliness. Serving as a "mirror of scorn and pity towards Man", which Tolkien considered one of the chief characteristics of all good fairy stories,[1] Scrooge has shone across the generations as a beacon of hope and redemption, as powerful parabolically as the prodigal son of which he is a type.

The story begins with the cold hard fact that Jacob Marley is "as dead as a door-nail":

> There is no doubt that Marley was dead. This must be distinctly understood, or nothing wonderful can come of the story I am going to relate. If we were not perfectly convinced that Hamlet's Father died before the play began, there would be nothing more remarkable in his taking a

---

[1] J. R. R. Tolkien, *Tree and Leaf* (London: Unwin, 1988), p. 28.

stroll at night, in an easterly wind, upon his own ramparts, than there would be in any other middle-aged gentleman rashly turning out after dark in a breezy spot ... literally to astonish his son's weak mind.[2]

The connection with *Hamlet* at the very beginning of the novella has a deep significance that the whimsical tone should not obscure. In Shakespeare's play as in Dickens' story the ghosts serve to introduce not merely a supernatural dimension to the work but a supernatural perception of reality. The ghosts reveal what is hidden to mortal eyes. They see more. They serve as supernatural messengers who reveal crimes that would otherwise have remained hidden. Their intervention is necessary for reality to be seen and understood and for justice to be done. Thus, in connecting Jacob Marley's ghost to the ghost of Hamlet's father, Dickens is indicating the role and purpose of the ghosts that he will introduce to Scrooge, and to us. They will show us not only Scrooge but ourselves in a manner that has the power to surprise us out of our own worldliness and to open us to the spiritual realities that we are prone to forget.

It is, however, not only the ghosts who teach us timely and timeless lessons but our mortal neighbors also. It is, after all, worth remembering that the first visitors that Scrooge receives are not ghosts but men. His nephew waxes lyrical on what might be termed the magic or miracle of Christmas:

> I have always thought of Christmas time, when it has come round—apart from the veneration due to its sacred

[2] Charles Dickens, *A Christmas Carol: A Ghost Story of Christmas* (London: Chapman & Hall, 1843; Project Gutenberg, 2018), stave 2, "Marley's Ghost", https://www.gutenberg.org/files/46/46-h/46-h.htm.

name and origin, if anything belonging to it can be apart from that—as a good time; a kind, forgiving, charitable, pleasant time; the only time I know of, in the long calendar of the year, when men and women seem by one consent to open their shut-up hearts freely, and to think of people below them as if they really were fellow-passengers to the grave, and not another race of creatures bound on other journeys.[3]

There is no need to remind Scrooge's nephew of the necessity of keeping Christ in Christmas! He knows that it is venerated because of its sacred name, *Christ-Mass*, and because of its sacred origin in the birth of the Savior. How can anything associated with Christmas be separated from its sacred source and purpose? The very thought, as expressed in the nephew's afterthought, is plainly absurd. Scrooge, ironically, does not disagree. He has no intention of celebrating the feast while ignoring its sacred name and origin as do most people in our own hedonistic times. He does not want to celebrate it at all. After complaining that his nephew should let him keep Christmas in his own way, the nephew reminds him that he doesn't keep it at all. "Let me leave it alone, then,"[4] Scrooge replies.

The other facet of the nephew's defense of Christmas that should not go unnoticed or unheeded is his reminder to his uncle that the poor and destitute are "fellow-passengers to the grave, and not another race of creatures bound on other journeys". This is not merely a *memento mori*, which, for the Christian, should always be a reminder of the Four Last Things—death, judgment, heaven, and hell—but is a reminder that we are not *homo sapiens*, smug in the presumption of our cleverness, but

[3] Ibid.
[4] Ibid.

homo viator, creatures or "passengers" on the journey of life, the only purpose of which is to get to heaven. Furthermore, our fellow travelers, sanctified by their being made in God's image, are our mystical equals, irrespective of their social or economic status, whom we are commanded to love. They are not "another race of creatures bound on other journeys" but are our very kith and kin bound on the same journey of life as we are. The inescapable truth, inextricably bound to the great commandment of Christ that we love the Lord our God and that we love our neighbor (see Matthew 22:37–38), is that we cannot reach the destination that is the very purpose of life's journey without helping our fellow travelers get there with us. The lesson that *A Christmas Carol* teaches is that our lives are not *owned* by us but are *owed* to another to whom the debt must be paid in the currency of self-sacrifice, which is love's means of exchange.

A Christmas Carol is, therefore, as might be expected of a meditation on the spirit of Christmas, a literary work that operates most profoundly on the level of theology.

Let's conclude our own meditation on this most wonderful of stories with a further consideration of its theological dimension, especially with regard to the nature or supernature of the ghosts. Marley's ghost, like the ghost of Hamlet's father, is presumably a soul in purgatory and not one of the damned. This would appear to be evident from the ghost's penitential and avowedly Christian spirit and its desire to save Scrooge from following in its folly-laden footsteps. When Scrooge seeks to console him with the reminder that he had always been "a good man of business", Marley's ghost wrings its hands in conscience-driven agitation. "Business!" he cries. "Mankind was my business. The common welfare was my business; charity, mercy, forbearance, and benevolence, were, all, my business. The dealings of my trade were but a drop of water in the comprehensive ocean of my business!"[5]

If Marley's ghost is the spirit of a mortal man, suffering penitentially and purgatorially for its sins, the Ghosts of Christmases Past, Present, and Yet to Come are best described as angels. They are divine messengers (*angelos*, in Greek, means messenger). More specifically, they might be seen as Scrooge's own guardian angels, as can be seen from the first Ghost's description of himself as being the Ghost of Scrooge's own past.

The final aspect of *A Christmas Carol* that warrants mention, especially in light of its poignant pertinence to our own meretricious times, is its celebration of life in general and the lives of large families in particular. The burgeoning family of Bob Cratchit—in spite of its poverty, or dare we say because of it—is the very hearth and home from which the warmth of life and love glows through the pages of Dickens' story. At the very heart of that hearth and home is the blessed life of the disabled child, Tiny Tim, which shines forth in Tiny Tim's love for others and in the love that his family has for him. His very presence is the light of caritas that serves catalytically to bring Scrooge to his senses. After his conversion, Scrooge no longer sees the poor and disabled as being surplus to the needs of the population who should be allowed to die—as in our own day, they are routinely killed or culled in the womb—but as a blessing to be cherished and praised. For this love of life, even of the life of the disabled, *especially* of the life of the disabled, is at the heart of everyone who knows the true spirit of Christmas as exemplified in the helplessness of the Babe of Bethlehem. "And so, as Tiny Tim observed, God bless Us, Every One!"[6]

---

[5] Ibid.
[6] Ibid., stave 5, "The End of It".

Chapter Nine

The Picture of Dorian Gray

Oscar Wilde wrote several first-rate plays, on which his literary reputation principally rests, and a number of mostly second-rate poems. He is also lauded, quite rightly, for his short stories, mainly for children, of which "The Selfish Giant" and "The Canterville Ghost" warrant special mention. He wrote only one novel, *The Picture of Dorian Gray*, which is one of the finest of a literary golden age that G. K. Chesterton celebrated in *The Victorian Age in Literature*.

It is not possible to understand the conflicting passions at the troubled heart of Wilde's novel without understanding the conflicting passions at the heart of its troubled author. Oscar Wilde was a deeply flawed genius who was lauded for his genius and loathed for his flaws. He was one of the most celebrated wits of late Victorian England and probably the most popular playwright of his generation. Yet he was also held in scorn for his dandyism and his decadence and was perceived by many as a corrupter of public morals. At the same time, his works, for the most part, exhibit a profoundly orthodox Christian morality. From the charm of his fairy stories to the denouements of his plays, Wilde shows himself to be a Christian writer par excellence. How can we make sense of these apparent contradictions, and how will this help us to understand the deepest meaning of his novel?

What indeed are we to make of this most beguiled and beguiling, this most confused and confusing of men? How do we set about resolving the riddle that Wilde sets us? Does he have anything of value to teach us? Is his work of relevance to our own times? Is his art an icon, revealing the image of Christ and His truth to the world, or is it iconoclastic, seeking to tear down moral conventions with decadent abandon? Ask these questions of the average postmodern intellectual and you will probably be told that Wilde was a brilliant artist who was persecuted for his homosexuality and deserves to be remembered as a martyr for the cause of sexual "liberation" who was sacrificed on the altar of puritanical Victorian values. Ask the same question of someone who knows the real facts of Wilde's life and you will be told that Wilde was a brilliant artist (the "intellectual" gets that part of the story right, at least) who was never at peace with his homosexuality and who, when at last faced with the sordid reality of his situation, described his homosexual predilections as his "pathology".

The first thing we need to know about Wilde is that he was at war with himself. Wilde the would-be saint and Wilde the woeful sinner were in deadly conflict, one with the other. In this he was no different from the rest of us. Throughout his life, even at those times that he was at his most "decadent", he retained a deep love for the Person of Christ and a lasting reverence for the Catholic Church. Born in Dublin in 1854, of Irish Protestant parents, Wilde spent much of his life flirting with Catholicism. He almost converted as an undergraduate at Trinity College in Dublin and was on the brink of conversion a year or so later as an undergraduate at Magdalen College, Oxford. There were no doctrinal differences preventing him from being received into the Church. He believed everything the Church believed and even spoke eloquently and wittily in defense of Catholic dogmas such as the Immaculate Conception. The only reason he failed to follow the logic of his Catholic convictions was a fear of being disinherited by his father if he did so. Years later, after his fall from favor following the scandal surrounding his homosexual affair with Lord Alfred Douglas, he spoke wistfully of his reluctant decision to turn his back on the Church. "Much of my moral obliquity is due to the fact that my father would not allow me to become a Catholic," he confided to a journalist. "The artistic side of the Church would have cured my degeneracies. I intend to be received before long."[1] In the event, he was finally received into the Church shortly before his death in 1900.

Wilde would not have been happy with the manner in which his literary achievement has been partially eclipsed by the sordid and squalid details of his private life. "You knew what my Art was to me," he wrote to Lord Alfred Douglas, his "friend" and nemesis, "the great primal note by which I had revealed, first myself to myself, and then myself to the world; the real passion of my life; the love to which all other loves were as marsh-water to red wine."[2] As he died in disgraced exile, in Paris, in garret poverty, he must have feared that future generations would see only the marsh-water of his murky "loves", leaving the wine of his art untasted.

The wine of Wilde's art was fermented in the Christianity that informed the moral dimension of his work. His poetry exhibits either a selfless love for Christ or, at its darkest, a deep self-loathing in the face of the ugliness of his own sinfulness. His short stories are almost always

[1] H. Montgomery Hyde, *Oscar Wilde: A Biography* (London: Eyre Methuen, 1976), p. 368.

[2] De Profundis, letter from Reading Gaol to Lord Alfred Douglas by Oscar Wilde, autograph (London: British Library, Department of Manuscripts).

animated by a deep Christian morality, with "The Selfish Giant" deserving a timeless accolade as one of the finest Christian fairy stories ever written. His plays are more than merely comedies or tragedies; they are morality plays in which virtue is vindicated and vice vanquished. And this brings us to *The Picture of Dorian Gray*, Wilde's only novel and a true masterpiece of Victorian fiction.

From the outset, we are confronted and perhaps affronted by the provocative Preface with which Wilde raises the curtain on his novel. It says something of the power of Wilde's aphoristic wit, which was the toast of the salons of London and Paris prior to his downfall, that the two-page Preface is almost as well-known as the novel itself and that it almost outshines it in brilliance. Take, for example, Wilde's vituperatively splenetic judgment on his own age:

> *The nineteenth century dislike of realism is the rage of Caliban seeing his own face in a glass.*
>
> *The nineteenth century dislike of romanticism is the rage of Caliban not seeing his own face in a glass.*[3]

For Wilde, late Victorian England is synonymous with Caliban, the monstrous subhuman character in Shakespeare's *The Tempest* who is bereft of all culture, all civilized values, and all Christian virtues. Caliban's physical deformity is a reflection of his moral and spiritual ugliness, whose very name, effectively an anagram of *cannibal*, cries out against him. Such an age hates realism because it cannot bear to see the ugly truth about itself, but it also hates romanticism because it refuses to see the existence of a beauty beyond its own ugliness. An age that can't bear to look at itself and can't bear to look beyond itself is in trouble!

---

[3] *Picture of Dorian Gray*, ed. Joseph Pearce, Ignatius Critical Editions (San Francisco: Ignatius Press, 2008), p. 3.

Having held up a Swiftian mirror of satirical scorn to his own age, revealing its ugliness, he praises those who are open to the gifts of beauty.

Those who find ugly meanings in beautiful things are corrupt without being charming. This is a fault.

Those who find beautiful meanings in beautiful things are the cultivated. For these there is hope.[4]

This emphatically nonrelativistic emphasis on the objective presence of beauty, which is not in the eye of the beholder but is present in spite of the beholder's ability to see it, serves as a condemnation of the blindness of cynicism that cannot see beauty even when it is shown it, perceiving only ugliness. One is reminded of a line from one of Wilde's plays in which a cynic is defined as one who sees the price of everything and the value of nothing. The cynic is a relativist who cannot see that which is intrinsically beautiful, a thing's inherent value, but only that which is subject to the fluctuations of his own fleeting feelings, the price that he assigns to it at any given time and that is always subject to change.

Thus far, Wilde is revealing himself in the Preface to his novel as a tradition-oriented aesthete, reflecting his long-standing preference for the traditionalist aesthetic of John Ruskin over that of the modernist Walter Pater, both of whom had influenced him deeply in his formative years at Oxford. The problem is that this traditionalist aesthetic is largely ignored by modern critics who prefer to accentuate Wilde's claim in the same Preface that art is beyond morality.

[4] Ibid.

*There is no such thing as a moral or an immoral book. Books are
well written, or badly written. That is all.*[5]

This elevation of beauty over morality does violence to
the traditional transcendental synthesis of the good, the true,
and the beautiful, which Christian philosophers have rightly
connected to the Trinity itself. To separate the beautiful from
the good (virtue) and the true (reason) is to do violence to
the cosmos itself. To split the Trinity of the transcendentals
is the ontological equivalent of splitting the atom, as explosive and as destructive metaphysically as the atom bomb is
physically. It is no wonder that Wilde's iconoclastic bomb,
dropped with seeming nonchalance into the midst of his
Preface, is quoted *ad nauseam* by those seeking the nihilistic
destruction and deconstruction of meaning itself.

There is, however, a delicious irony in the fact that
Wilde flagrantly denies and defies his own aphorism in the
writing of the novel, in which he presents in the denouement of the plot a vision of morality that is profoundly
Christian and that seems to prophesy his own eventual
conversion. In essence, following the Faustian tradition,
Wilde tells the story of a man (Dorian Gray) who, inspired
by his own vanity and by the iconoclastic philosophy of his
satanic tempter (Lord Henry Wotton), sells his soul to the
devil in return for the retention of his boyish good looks.
As Gray indulges his sensual appetites with an increasingly
insatiable hunger, his portrait grows uglier and more cruel,
a mirror of the corruption of his soul.

In the midst of Gray's descent into ever-deepening pits of
depravity, he is given a "yellow book" by Lord Henry Wotton, which, from the description that Wilde gives of its lurid
plot, is quite obviously Huysmans' decadent masterpiece, *À
Rebours*, a novel that depicts the protagonist's life of sheer

[5] Ibid.

sensual self-indulgence—leading, via ennui, to an ultimate scream of despair and a desperate desire for God. Wilde's protagonist follows the same downward path, except that Dorian Gray refuses to repent. Instead, he begins to despise the portrait, which is now hideously grotesque and spattered with the blood that he had spilled. Seeing the painting as a reflection of his conscience and indeed as a reflection of his soul, he decides to destroy it so that he might enjoy his sins without the painting's hideous reminder of their consequences. His effort to destroy it proves fatal, indeed suicidal. The moral, as inescapable as it is clear, is that the killing of the conscience is the killing of the soul and that the killing of the soul is the killing of the self.

Where does this leave Wilde's claim that there is no such thing as a moral or an immoral book? Wilde himself answers the question with his own emphatic insistence that *Dorian Gray* is a moral book. Responding to a negative review of his newly published novel in the *St. James Gazette* in June 1890, Wilde wrote the following defense of its deepest moral meaning:

> All excess, as well as all renunciation, brings its own punishment. The painter, Basil Hallward, worshipping physical beauty far too much, as most painters do, dies by the hand of one in whose soul he has created a monstrous and absurd vanity. Dorian Gray, having led a life of mere sensation and pleasure, tries to kill conscience, and at that moment kills himself. Lord Henry Wotton seeks to be merely the spectator of life. He finds that those who reject the battle are more deeply wounded than those who take part in it. Yes; there is a terrible moral in *Dorian Gray*—a moral which the prurient will not be able to find in it, but which will be revealed to all whose minds are healthy. Is this an artistic error? I fear it is. It is the only error in the book.[6]

[6] *St. James Gazette*, June 26, 1890.

This short defense of the morality of the work is of particular importance because it is the most direct comment on the novel's meaning by the author himself. Clearly, Wilde considered *Dorian Gray* to be a moral book and that the moral was so obvious and unsubtle that it constituted "an artistic error". The work would have been better, artistically, if he had subsumed or hidden the moral a little more subtly within the story rather than allowing it to stick out like a spike. Although the novel's morality will be evident to all those who read it with a healthy mind, the unhealthy, such as the prurient, will not be able to see the moral of the story, even if it's literarily staring them in the face. Blinded by the ignorance of their ignobility, they grub around among the novel's sordid details with salacious abandon or puritanical disdain, flailing about in the darkness and failing to perceive the light. Missing the point, they impale themselves on something else. Here we shall leave them flailing hopelessly, while we look with Wilde at the deeper morality of the work.

The Picture of Dorian Gray was first published in *Lippincott's Magazine* in 1890 and was published in book form with additional chapters and a Preface in the following year. Its principal protagonists are Lord Henry Wotton and Dorian Gray, the former being the primary cause of the latter's corruption through a poisonous influence akin to infernal possession: "He would seek to dominate him— had already, indeed, half done so. He would make that wonderful spirit his own."[7]

Lord Henry at first confuses and then converts the youthful Gray to his gospel of decadence, flattering Dorian's vanity and tempting him to self-indulgence:

[7] *Picture of Dorian Gray*, p. 41.

The mutilation of the savage has its tragic survival in the self-denial that mars our lives. We are punished for our refusals. Every impulse that we strive to strangle broods in the mind and poisons us. The body sins once, and has done with its sin, for action is a mode of purification. Nothing remains then but the recollection of a pleasure, or the luxury of a regret. The only way to get rid of a temptation is to yield to it.[8]

Poisoned by Lord Henry's flattery and philandering philosophy, Dorian's vanity verges on the insanity that will ultimately cause both suicide and murder. "I know, now", he exclaims to Basil Hallward, the artist who had painted his portrait,

> that when one loses one's good looks ... one loses everything. Your picture has taught me that. Lord Henry Wotton is perfectly right. Youth is the only thing worth having. When I find that I am growing old, I shall kill myself....
>
> I am jealous of everything whose beauty does not die. I am jealous of the portrait you have painted of me. Why should it keep what I must lose? Every moment that passes takes something from me, and gives something to it. Oh, if it were only the other way! If the picture could change, and I could be always what I am now! Why did you paint it? It will mock me some day—mock me horribly!"[9]

This is the catastrophic point upon which the whole novel rests. The moment of truth. Significantly, Wilde suggests a supernatural element. As soon as these words are spoken, Dorian throws himself onto the divan, burying his face in the cushions, "as though he were praying". Thus, with

[8] Ibid., p. 22.
[9] Ibid., pp. 30–31.

hints of either the divine or the diabolical, Dorian's wish receives added power. Whether from prayer to God or through a pact with the devil, his wish will be granted. The portents of doom are suggested in the prophetic nature of Dorian's final words. The picture will indeed mock him horribly one day, but only because it has faithfully reflected his desire that it change while he remains the same.

Dorian's desire for eternal youth keeps him outwardly beautiful, but the price he pays is an inner corruption. The picture grows increasingly ugly with every act of sin and cruelty that Dorian commits. When he commits murder, the hands of the picture drip with blood. Dorian's physical beauty is but a mask, ultimately superficial. The metaphysical reality is to be found in the portrait, which becomes the mirror of his soul, the ugly truth staring him uncomfortably in the face.

The novel's plot unfurls like a parable, illuminating the grave spiritual dangers involved in a life of immoral action and experiment. Its ante-climax—the lesser climax that precedes its ultimate moral—is an angry exchange between Dorian Gray and Basil Hallward. The artist beseeches his friend to deny all the horrible stories that are circulating about him. Dorian smiles contemptuously and decides to show Hallward the hideously deformed painting that he has locked away from prying eyes in an upstairs room. "Come upstairs, Basil. . . . I keep a diary of my life from day to day, and it never leaves the room in which it is written. I shall show it to you if you come with me."[10]

"So you think that it is only God who sees the soul, Basil?" Dorian asks before revealing the picture.

An exclamation of horror broke from the painter's lips as he saw in the dim light the hideous face on the canvas

[10] Ibid., p. 169.

grinning at him. There was something in its expression
that filled him with disgust and loathing. Good heavens!
it was Dorian Gray's own face that he was looking at! ...
   "It is the face of my soul", Dorian explains.[11]

Examining the portrait, which he himself had painted
many years earlier, Hallward sees that "the leprosies of sin
were slowly eating the thing away." Immediately, we are
reminded that Dorian Gray's life is worse than any death:
"The rotting of a corpse in a watery grave was not so
fearful." What follows is surely an example of the overt
Christian morality that had prompted Wilde to lament
the "artistic error" that had made the moral of his novel
too obvious: "Good God, Dorian, what a lesson! What an
awful lesson! ... Pray, Dorian, pray.... The prayer of your
pride has been answered. The prayer of your repentance
will be answered also."[12]

Believing that he too is being punished for his idolatrous
love for Dorian, Hallward beseeches his friend to join him
in prayers of penance. Dorian appears to be teetering on
the brink of repentance when "an uncontrollable feeling
of hatred for Basil Hallward came over him, as though it
had been suggested to him by the image on the canvas".[13]
Grabbing a knife he stabs the artist repeatedly in the neck
until he is dead, thereby adding murder to the catalogue of
sins that he had committed.

The wretchedness of Dorian's life becomes ever more
pronounced as the novel approaches its climax. When
one of his former dalliances, now a prostitute, calls him
"the devil's bargain", he reacts angrily as if stabbed by
the truth of the words. Finally, the novel's overarching
moral, implicit throughout, is stated explicitly in Dorian's

[11] Ibid., pp. 171–72.
[12] Ibid., pp. 172–73.
[13] Ibid., p. 173.

last conversation with Lord Henry. "By the way, Dorian," Lord Henry asks, no doubt intent on observing his quarry's reaction, " 'what does it profit a man if he gain the whole world and lose'—how does the quotation run?— 'his own soul'?" Startled by the question, Dorian stares in horror at his friend: "Why do you ask me that, Harry?"

"My dear fellow," says Lord Henry, elevating his eyebrows in feigned surprise, "I asked you because I thought you might be able to give me an answer. That is all."[14]

Lord Henry proceeds to mock the whole concept of the soul's existence, proclaiming that art has a soul but man has not. Faced with such facile posturing, Dorian offers the fruits of his own bitter experience: "The soul is a terrible reality. It can be bought, and sold, and bartered away. It can be poisoned, or made perfect. There is a soul in each one of us. I know it."[15]

With his own sin, and Lord Henry's cynicism, weighing heavily on his conscience, Dorian feels "a wild longing for the unstained purity of his boyhood". He compares his own wretchedness with the innocence of the latest woman whom "he had lured to love him". "What a laugh she had!—just like a thrush singing. And how pretty she had been in her cotton dresses and her large hats! She knew nothing, but she had everything that he had lost."[16] It is difficult to read and ponder such lines without an image of the "unstained purity" of Eden springing to mind. The innocent girl, as yet untainted and unsullied by Dorian's deadly touch, reminds us of Eve. She has not yet eaten from the tree of the knowledge of good and evil from which Dorian had glutted himself insatiably:

[14] Ibid., pp. 233–34.
[15] Ibid., p. 234.
[16] Ibid., p. 239.

He knew that he had tarnished himself, filled his mind with corruption and given horror to his fancy; that he had been an evil influence on others, and had experienced a terrible joy in being so; and that, of the lives that had crossed his own, it had been the fairest and the most full of promise that he had brought to shame.…

Ah! in what a monstrous moment of pride and passion he had prayed that the portrait should bear the burden of his days, and he keep the unsullied splendour of eternal youth! All his failure had been due to that. Better for him that each sin of his life had been brought its sure, swift penalty along with it. There was purification in punishment.[17]

Such contemplation brings Dorian to the very brink of repentance but, at the last, he feels unable to confess his sins, unwilling to accept the consequences of his crimes. If he cannot cleanse his soul from sin, he must be rid of the conscience that has made his sins a burden to him. Then, liberated from any trace of conscience, he can once more enjoy his sinful life. Convinced that the hideous portrait is to blame, he decides upon its destruction. "It had been like a conscience to him. Yes, it had been conscience. He would destroy it."[18] In the novel's final climactic moments, we see the fulfillment of the moral that Wilde himself had ascribed to his novel, that "in his attempt to kill conscience Dorian Gray kills himself".[19]

In spite of Wilde's claim in the Preface to the novel that there was no such thing as a moral book, there can be little doubt that The Picture of Dorian Gray is itself a contradiction of the claim. Few novels have been more obviously moral in extent and intent than this cautionary tale of a

[17] Ibid., pp. 239–40.
[18] Ibid., p. 242.
[19] St. James Gazette, June 26, 1890.

soul's betrayal of itself and others. Wilde himself insisted, in the face of further claims that the book was immoral, that "it is a story with a moral" and that the moral possessed an "ethical beauty".[20] He also insisted, once again, that the novel's weakness was not in the absence of a moral but in its all too obvious presence:

> The real trouble I experienced in writing the story was that of keeping the extremely obvious moral subordinate to the artistic and dramatic effect.
>
> When I first conceived the idea of a young man selling his soul in exchange for eternal youth—an idea that is old in the history of literature, but to which I have given new form—I felt that, from an aesthetic point of view, it would be difficult to keep the moral in its proper secondary place; and even now I do not feel quite sure that I have been able to do so. I think the moral too apparent.[21]

Amid the condemnation of many secular critics of the "immoral" nature of the novel, a few eyebrows were raised by the praise that it received from several Christian publications. *Christian Leader* and the *Christian World* referred to it as an ethical parable, and *Light*, a journal of Christian mysticism, regarded it as "a work of high spiritual import". A critic in the *Scots Observer* who had previously attacked the novel scathingly commented sarcastically that it must have been "particularly painful" for Wilde to discover that his work was being praised by Christian publications on both sides of the Atlantic. Wilde, however, appeared to be pleased by Christian approval of the morality of his novel, insisting that he had

> no hesitation in saying that I regard such criticism as a very gratifying tribute to my story.

[20] Ibid.
[21] *Daily Chronicle*, July 2, 1890.

For if a work of art is rich, and vital, and complete, those who have artistic instincts will see its beauty, and those to whom ethics appeal more strongly than aesthetics will see its moral lesson. It will fill the cowardly with terror, and the unclean will see in it their own shame. It will be to each man what he is himself. It is the spectator, and not life, that art really mirrors.[22]

This appraisal by Wilde of art in general, and his own work in particular, is singularly intriguing because it suggests that he believes that his novel serves the reader in the same way that the portrait serves Dorian Gray, as a mirror that reflects the state of one's soul. The implications for the reader of *Dorian Gray* are obvious. We can, if we choose, learn from the moral lessons that it teaches and apply it to our own lives.

Writing to a friend within weeks of the novel's publication, Wilde complained that "it has been attacked on ridiculous grounds, but I think it will be ultimately recognized as a real work of art with a strong ethical lesson inherent in it".[23]

Ironically, one of the most poignant appraisals of *The Picture of Dorian Gray* was made, many years later, by Lord Alfred Douglas, whose homosexual relationship with Wilde would tarnish the writer's reputation far more conclusively than any of his books. In his memoirs, Douglas attacked those Victorian critics who had condemned *Dorian Gray* for being immoral as well as the later generations of critics who attacked its morality:

As a matter of fact the book is entirely moral, and that is probably why the feeble and the sheep-like critics of today affect to despise it.... What they do not like about

[22] *Scots Observer*, August 2, 1890.
[23] Arthur Fish, "Memories of Oscar Wilde", *Cassell's Weekly*, May 2, 1923.

Dorian Gray is precisely that it is the moral story of a man who destroys his own conscience and thereby comes to a terrible end. If Dorian Gray had been presented as triumphant and "happy" to the last, they would probably hail it as a great work of art, whereas Oscar Wilde, just like Shakespeare or any first-rate writer, knew that a play or a novel without a moral is, from the artistic point of view, a monstrosity.

I once said ... that while *Dorian Gray* was on the surface a moral book, there was in it "an undercurrent of immorality and corruption". I said that out of the bitterness of my heart, but it was not a fair criticism, because the "undercurrent" is part of the legitimate atmosphere which the author creates for his story.[24]

These words, written almost fifty years after the novel's publication, suggest that Wilde's stricture in the Preface to *Dorian Gray* that there was no such thing as a moral or an immoral book had been contradicted by almost everyone who read it, and indeed by the one who wrote it. The issue of morality was as central to critical conceptions and misconceptions of the book as it had been to the author's own conceptions of it. Wilde's own attitude to the critics of his novel was best summarized in the lesser known but more profound aphorism from the Preface that we quoted earlier: "Those who find ugly meanings in beautiful things are corrupt without being charming. This is a fault. Those who find beautiful meanings in beautiful things are the cultivated. For these there is hope." And let's not forget that Wilde, in his own appraisal of the novel, confirmed his belief in this lesser known aphorism in his insistence that "there is a terrible moral in *Dorian Gray*—a moral

[24] Lord Alfred Douglas, *Without Apology* (London: Martin Secker, 1938), pp. 41–43.

which the prurient will not be able to find in it, but which will be revealed to all whose minds are healthy".[25]

Wilde's words are a challenge to every reader of *The Picture of Dorian Gray*. If the reader approaches the work in the critically cultivated manner that Wilde prescribes, there is indeed hope that he will learn the priceless lesson that Wilde teaches. Like all good art, of which the portrait in the novel is itself a powerful symbol, *The Picture of Dorian Gray* holds up a mirror to its readers. It shows us ourselves and teaches us the terrible lessons that we need to learn.

There are indeed such things as moral and immoral books, whether well written or badly written. Moral books show us ourselves and our place in the cosmos. They are epiphanies of grace. Immoral books are like Lord Henry Wotton in Wilde's story or indeed like the devil himself in the story in which we are all living. They are liars and deceivers who show us a false picture of ourselves and the world in which we live. Moral books wake us up; immoral books lull us to sleep. *The Picture of Dorian Gray* wakes us up, stirring us from the somnambulant path of least resistance that leads to hell. It is for this reason, if for no other, that we should thank heaven for the vision of hell that Wilde's novel reveals to us.

[25] *St. James Gazette*, June 26, 1890.

Chapter Ten

The Man Who Was Thursday

G.K. Chesterton had a low opinion of his own abilities as a novelist. He confessed,

> My real judgment of my own work is that I have spoilt a number of jolly good ideas in my time. I think *The Napoleon of Notting Hill* was a book very well worth writing; but I am not sure that it was ever written. I think that a harlequinade like *The Flying Inn* was an extremely promising subject, but I very strongly doubt whether I kept the promise. I am almost tempted to say that it is still a very promising subject—for somebody else.[1]

He thought *The Ball and the Cross* had "quite a good plot", based on "a social suggestion that really has a great deal in it; but I am much more doubtful about whether I got a great deal out of it". Although as stories or "anecdotes", his fictional works were "fresh and personal", "considered as novels, they were not only not as good as a real novelist would have made them, but they were not as good as I might have made them myself, if I had really even been trying to be a real novelist".[2] Considering that Chesterton prefaced this confession of failure with an explicit denial that he was indulging in

---

[1] G.K. Chesterton, *Autobiography* (New York: Sheed & Ward, 1936), p. 297.
[2] Ibid., p. 298.

"mock modesty", we have little option but to believe that this was indeed his "real judgment" on his own fictional work. This places the admirer of Chesterton's novels in an awkward position. Do we question Chesterton's judgment or, eating humble pie, do we question our own?

Although eating humble pie is good for us, providing healthy spiritual nourishment, we are nonetheless at liberty to seek further clarification of the reasons for Chesterton's self-deprecatory judgment. Such is provided in his conclusion that he was not able to be a novelist because he had always been a journalist. The fact is that Chesterton wrote everything in haste, as a spontaneous outpouring of his genial and ingenious muse. He wrote his novels in the same manner in which he wrote his essays, at breathtaking speed on the wings of wit and wisdom. One suspects that he seldom stopped to catch his breath, or to check his facts, as the flow of words poured forth from his pen. This makes for exhilarating and oft-times exhausting reading, but it also leads, especially in his longer works of fiction, to a degree of negligence with regard to formal considerations of plot consistency and character development. It is for this reason that reading one of Chesterton's novels is like riding a ramshackle rollercoaster, so loosely constructed that it seems to teeter on the brink of collapse! And yet we ride the rollercoaster, in spite of our more pedantic prejudices, because we are doing so in the presence of an indefatigably rambunctious genius. Only a fool would not want to ride such a rollercoaster!

Having agreed with Chesterton's negative judgment of his own novels (without eating humble pie!), it is nonetheless intriguing that *The Man Who Was Thursday*, which is probably the best of his novels and certainly the best known, is omitted from the novels that he dismisses. What, one wonders, is the reason for this? Is it a mere oversight or is it perhaps a conscious omission? Either way, it seems a little odd that Chesterton should forget or omit to mention his best known and most celebrated novel in his self-effacing and self-deprecating dismissal of his oeuvre. Dare we believe that the best of his novels was omitted because Chesterton, believing it to be his best, did not feel that it warranted the same dismissive treatment as the others? Might we believe that it was not a sin of omission but a virtuous omission, much as T. S. Eliot significantly omits Rome from the list of "unreal cities" in *The Waste Land*:

> Falling towers
> Jerusalem Athens Alexandria
> Vienna London
> Unreal

Eliot's omission of the Eternal City from the list of "falling towers" screams in the vacuum created by its absence, drawing attention to the fact that, unlike these other edifices of civilization, Rome is real and not destined to fall. Does Chesterton's omission of *Thursday* scream at us in the same way? Does he wish us to take it seriously as a work of literary art? My guess is that he does, and I believe that we should.

Although *Thursday* suffers from the same formal negligence that afflicts Chesterton's other novels, a fact that the author admits in his description of it as a "formless form of a piece of fiction",[3] it grapples so grippingly with the philosophical follies of the zeitgeist, and with such brio and brilliance, that it demands a place in the canon of great works.

As we begin to delve deeper into this darkest and yet lightest of novels, we should begin with the voice of

---

[3] Ibid., p. 98.

authority, which is to say with the voice of the author. In his autobiography, written at the end of his life and therefore serving as his final judgment, Chesterton discussed the novel's title and, most significantly, its subtitle:

> The title attracted some attention at the time; and there were many journalistic jokes about it. Some, referring to my supposed festive views, affected to mistake it for "The Man Who Was Thirsty". Others naturally supposed that Man Thursday was the black brother of Man Friday. Others again, with more penetration, treated it as a mere title out of topsy-turvydom; as if it had been "The Woman Who Was Half-past Eight", or "The Cow Who Was Tomorrow Evening". But what interests me about it was this; that hardly anybody who looked at the title ever seems to have looked at the sub-title: which was "A Nightmare," and the answer to a good many critical questions.[4]

If, therefore, the critic would like to have his questions answered about this most beguiling and confusing of novels, he needs to see it as a dark and dismal dreamscape, predating and perhaps prophesying the rise of surrealism, though very different from surrealism in its inspirational source and in its solution to the problems posed by the psychological subjectivism that it confronts.

The novel's inspirational source was Chesterton's own experience of the decadence of the 1890s and his recoiling in horror from the radical pessimism of fashionable philosophers, such as Schopenhauer. Speaking in old age of his experience of such subjectivism as an impressionable young man, he wrote that "my eyes were turned inwards rather than outwards; giving my moral personality, I should imagine, a very unattractive squint":

[4] Ibid., p. 98.

I was still oppressed with the metaphysical nightmare of negations about mind and matter, with the morbid imagery of evil, with the burden of my own mysterious brain and body; but by this time I was in revolt against them; and trying to construct a healthier conception of cosmic life, even if it were one that should err on the side of health. I even called myself an optimist, because I was so horribly near to being a pessimist. It is the only excuse I can offer.[5]

These lines from his autobiography immediately precede Chesterton's discussion of *The Man Who Was Thursday*, indicating that the novel grew from the murkiness and mawkishness of the author's doubt-filled adolescence:

The whole story is a nightmare of things, not as they are, but as they seemed to the young half-pessimist of the '90s; and the ogre who appears brutal but is also cryptically benevolent is not so much God, in the sense of religion or irreligion, but rather Nature as it appears to the pantheist, whose pantheism is struggling out of pessimism. So far as the story had any sense in it, it was meant to begin with the picture of the world at its worst and to work towards the suggestion that the picture was not so black as it was already painted.[6]

Having paid due deference to the authorial voice and its inherent authority, we can now dare to question its veracity. Chesterton was writing this explication of his novel in the mid-1930s, shortly before his death, and was failing to place sufficient distance between the inspirational roots of the novel in the decadence and confusion of the early 1890s and his own virtuous and settled state of mind at the

[5] Ibid., pp. 97–98.
[6] Ibid., pp. 98–99.

time that the novel was actually written fifteen years later. Although *The Man Who Was Thursday* is *inspired* by the confusion of the *fin de siècle*, it *aspires* to dispel and disperse the clouds of despondency with the piercing light of Christian clarity and charity. It cannot be stressed enough that this critical distance between the *inspirational* and *aspirational* aspects of the novel is crucial to our understanding of it. *Thursday* was written at around the same time that Chesterton was also writing *Orthodoxy*, his masterpiece of Christian apologetics, both books being published in 1908, and it is perilous to our understanding of the former book if we fail to read it in the light of the latter.

The aging Chesterton, recalling *Thursday* in the light of the darkness of his youth across the span of forty years, makes the perilous mistake of seeing the dragon of decadence and not the knight in shining orthodoxy who slays it. Thus, in his autobiography, he writes that "the monstrous pantomime ogre who was called Sunday in the story ... is not so much God ... but rather Nature as it appears to the pantheist, whose pantheism is struggling out of pessimism", whereas, in fact, as the text testifies explicitly, Sunday refers to himself within the context of the Book of Genesis and the days of Creation as "the Sabbath" and "the peace of God", and, as if to hammer the point home, his final words are those of Christ Himself, asking his interlocutors, "Can ye drink of the cup that I drink of?" *Pace* Chesterton, whose myopic memory misreads his own novel, Sunday reveals himself as being much more than mere Nature, much more than a mere god: He reveals Himself as the Christian God, or at least as a manifestation of the Christian God, whose presence makes sense of the nightmare nonsense that His perceived absence presents.

Seeing *Thursday* in the contemporaneous light of *Orthodoxy* and its "ethics of elfland", we can see that it encapsulates the paradox, embodied in the character of Chesterton's delightful priest-detective Fr. Brown, that wisdom can only be found in innocence. This is nothing less than the truth that Christ teaches. We will not be with Him in heaven unless we become as little children.

The paradoxical heart of *The Man Who Was Thursday* is the tension that exists between the *childlikeness* demanded by Christ and the *childishness* that St. Paul tells us to avoid. We have to remain *childlike* by ceasing to be *childish*. The first is the wisdom of innocence, or the sanity of sanctity, whereby we see the miracle of life with eyes full of wonder; the second is the self-centerdness of one who refuses the challenge of growing up. Chesterton's *Man Who Was Thursday* is essentially about childish detectives attaining childlike wisdom, just as his later novel, *Manalive*, illustrates how the pure childlikeness of the aptly named Innocent Smith is misunderstood by the childish world in which he finds himself.

The Man Who Was Thursday shows us the paradoxical truth that it takes a big man to know how small he is. It shows us that thinking we are big is childish while knowing that we are small is childlike. Thinking we are big, the sin of pride, turns our world into a living nightmare. Knowing we are small wakes us up. In a world that is somnambulating deeper and deeper into the living nightmare it has made for itself, we are in more need than ever of the wide-awake awareness of G. K. Chesterton, a visionary who was larger than life because he spent his life on his knees.

Chapter Eleven

The Power and the Glory

Most Catholic readers of Graham Greene's *The Power and the Glory* are happy to accept the novel's Catholic credentials on the strength of its happy ending. The arrival of a new priest to replace the martyred whisky priest signifies the continuum of the faith and its resurrection. All's well that ends well, or so we are tempted to assume. It's almost as though the novelist is to be forgiven his theological and philosophical philandering throughout the novel because of the eutrophic climax that he presents to us at its end, much as the whisky priest is forgiven his manifold sins through his martyrdom. Like the deathbed penitent, the sins of the novelist are to be forgiven because of the good end he has made. But does such an ending absolve the novelist of all critical responsibility for his earlier sins of infidelity? Should we forgive and forget, or should we insist that the author remain responsible for any earlier faux pas in his work? Should we not remind ourselves, and the author, that a good end never justifies evil means? Such questions should animate any discussion of Greene's masterpiece, necessitating a closer scrutiny of the work as a whole irrespective of the virtuously climactic twist in its tail.

As with all literary criticism, an objective reading of the work requires an ability to see it through the eyes of the author, so far as this is possible. In seeing *The Power and*

the Glory through the eyes of Graham Greene, we perceive the whisky priest's almost demented impiety and antipiety as a reflection of Greene himself. It is, for instance,
hugely significant that Greene chose the following words
of Sir Thomas Browne, the seventeenth-century English
author, as an epigraph to his first novel, *The Man Within*:
"There's another man within me that's angry with me."
It's as though Greene is himself the angry man within his
characterization of the whisky priest, so much so that we
can almost see the priest as being demonically possessed
by the angry and angst-ridden ghost of the author himself. Throughout the duration of the work, this authorial
spirit whispers blasphemous thoughts into the protagonist's head, tempting him in the desert of his soul. Thus,
we see in *The Power and the Glory*, as in all of Greene's
work, a genuine groping for religious truth grappling with
the darkest recesses of the self-absorbed ego, the latter of
which is often expressed with self-obsessive Baudelairean
abandon. The consequence of such a struggle is the transposing of this darker side onto all of Greene's protagonists,
so that even their goodness is warped. Greene saw human
nature as "not black and white" but "black and grey",[1]
thereby implicitly denying the purity of the divine image
in man, and he referred to his need to write as "a neurosis
... an irresistible urge to pinch the abscess which grows
periodically in order to squeeze out all the pus".[2] Such a
neurotic Muse can hardly fail to convey something of its
own pathology in the very fabric of the work it creates.

    Unfortunately, the age of ignorance in which we find
ourselves is unable to distinguish morally between the

---

[1] Marie-Françoise Allain, *The Other Man: Conversations with Graham Greene*
(London: Bodley Head, 1983), p. 134.
    [2] Ibid., p. 149.

healthy and the pathological. In priding itself in having gone beyond good and evil, our age ceases to receive the succor of the former and succumbs to the succubus of the latter. It not only fails to see morality clearly; it fails to see it at all. Instead, it begins to see good as evil, and evil as good, becoming inverted infernally in the acceptance of the diabolical double entendres of Orwellian doublethink. This is crucial to our understanding of Greene's oeuvre because it helps us understand not only Greene's own tortured struggle with the paradoxes of faith but also the inability of many critics to understand his work in any objective sense. Take, for instance, the introduction to the Penguin Classics edition of *The Power and the Glory* in which the usually erudite John Updike opines that the novel "succeeds so resoundingly because there is something un-English about the Roman Catholicism which infuses, with its Manichaean darkness and tortured literalism, [Greene's] most ambitious fiction."[3] Updike's confusing and conflating of orthodoxy and heresy is symptomatic of the misreading of Greene's work by postmodern critics. Since the heresy of Manichaeism has been condemned and confuted by the Church, the employment of "Roman Catholicism" and "Manichaean darkness" as synonyms is oxymoronic. And yet, to be fair to Greene's critics, their confusion is due in large part to Greene's own conflation of heresy and orthodoxy. In other words, his novels are confusing because the author is confused. This being so, the best way of avoiding confusion in the reading of *The Power and the Glory* is to learn to see the ways in which Greene is confused, or, at least, the way that he willfully sows confusion in the minds and thoughts of his characters, thereby spreading

[3] John Updike, Introduction to *The Power and the Glory*, by Graham Greene, Penguin Classics (London: Penguin Classics, 2003), p. 29.

such confusion like a contagion to his readers. We only become immune to such contagion by being aware of the confusion. It is, therefore, necessary to reread the work with an eye to the error it contains, the reader becoming the whisky priest's confessor, calling attention to the priest's sins and demanding amendment, thereby succeeding where the novel's pathetic Padre José fails.

There is, of course, much that is good and laudable in the whisky priest, a goodness that is exemplified in the real if reluctant martyrdom that he endures throughout the length of the work. But even this goodness is polluted by the pus of Greene's creative neurosis. At the end of the first chapter, the priest feels an "unwilling hatred" of the child and the sick woman to whom he is going to minister the sacraments, blaming them for his missing of the ship that would have taken him to freedom. Hatred, like all disordered passion, is a disease of the will. It is not, and cannot be, "unwilling". It might become so ingrained and so habitual that it seems that we can do nothing about it; but all sin, in reality, can be overcome by the will's coop- eration with grace. Where there's a will, God provides the way.

A further example of Greene's tortured use of paradox is his characterization of the weak priest, Padre José, as a martyr. Unlike the priests who had chosen death or exile, Padre José had renounced his priesthood and was now liv- ing with his former housekeeper. Unhappy in his ménage, and dreading the regular duties of the marriage bed, he ruminates wistfully on his own fate compared to that of the priests who had lain down their lives for their faith: "He thought with envy of the men who had died: it was over so soon. They were taken up there to the cemetery and shot against the wall: in two minutes life was extinct. And they called that martyrdom. Here life went on and on; he was only sixty-two. He might live to ninety."[4] And so we see how the coward and equivocator, who serves, much to the cynical pleasure of the Marxist lieutenant, as a living cause of scandal to the Church and the priesthood, is seen as the true martyr, while those who had been killed for their faith had taken the easy or cowardly way out. If such ruminations are simply those of the dishonored priest, wallowing in self-pitying isolation, we can have no cause for complaint. But what if there is something of the morbidly playful and yet earnest voice of the author himself in these thoughts? What if Greene wants us really to consider Padre José as more of a martyr than those who had been killed for holding firm in their faith? If so, we must upbraid him for his error. It is true that the weak and treacherous priest is suffering greatly for his choices. Indeed, it is true that he might be suffering more than those who had died violent deaths for their faith. But suffering does not constitute virtue or martyrdom. If he is suffering for his own sinful actions, he is suffering the consequences of his own choices. Are those who suffer the pains of hell martyrs? Only Milton's Satan would answer such a question in the plaintive affirmative, and there is certainly something of the Miltonian satanic in the squirming twists of Greene's decidedly un-Chestertonian use of paradox. Greene's paradoxes, unlike Chesterton's, are not those of paradise but of *Paradise Lost*.

As we witness the woefully pathetic Padre José's final reluctant surrender to his wife's pleas that he "come to bed", we know that he himself has made the unwelcome bed in which he now must lie, and in which he must "lie" not only in the supine but in the perjurious sense of the word. He is living a lie and must suffer the consequences

---

[4] *Power and the Glory*, p. 29.

of his actions and the pangs of his conscience. We feel for him in his agony, even if he *is* culpable, and we sense the supernatural consequences of his choices. As the priest drags himself off to his loveless bed, "somebody somewhere laughed,"[5] and we feel that it is Satan himself who is laughing.

We learn later that Padre José is "in the grip of the unforgivable sin, despair",[6] and discover, in this choice of phrase, another of Greene's provocatively perverse paradoxes. The problem is that the desperate soul *refuses* forgiveness. In his pride, and we should not lose sight of the fact that despair is ultimately a sin of pride, the desperate soul believes that his sin and his hopelessness are beyond the forgiving power and fathomless love of the One who offers forgiveness and who has died for the sin. The desperate soul believes that his sin is too big, too grievous to be forgiven. The true paradox is not that despair is the unforgivable sin but that the despairing man lacks the *humility* to *hope* for forgiveness. Once again, we would have no cause for concern if the perverse paradox is only the product of Padre José's tortured and contorted conscience, a grievous error on his part that constitutes the very heart of his problem. Yet we suspect that the third-person narrative also contains more than a grain of the author's own contorted conception of truth. Such a suspicion is reinforced, and perhaps confirmed, a few pages later when we are informed that the novel's other priest and its principal protagonist had also "given way to despair—the unforgivable sin".[7] In this instance, the phrase appears in a long narrative section in which we can surely assume that the voice

[5] Ibid., p. 30.
[6] Ibid., p. 49.
[7] Ibid., p. 60.

is that of the narrator and not that of the whisky priest. In this theological playing with fire, Greene is dabbling and dappling with literary impressionism, blurring the voices of the narrator with that of his characters so that the author's voice blends indiscernibly with theirs. If this is so, the author shares in the errors that they espouse and commit. The result is what may be termed literary schizophrenia, in which it becomes impossible to distinguish the author's *objective* voice from the subjective voices of the characters in the text. The author loses himself in the plot and, in so doing, is in danger of losing the plot itself or losing his readers within it.

Another disturbing facet of the fictional narrative is the characterization of the whisky priest's illegitimate child. She is presented as being almost demonic, a "small malicious child"[8] who, utterly untamable, laughs sadistically at her father. She seems to be evil incarnate, possessed by the devil himself. "She knows her catechism ... but she won't say it,"[9] we are told by the child's mother. Such ingrained recalcitrance is confirmed by her spiteful defiance of the whisky priest's efforts to show her affection:

> He caught the look in the child's eyes which frightened him—it was again as if a grown woman was there before her time, making her plans, aware of far too much. It was like seeing his own mortal sin look back at him, without contrition.[10]

Clearly, the girl emerges here as a metaphor for the priest's sin of fornication, a fact that is reinforced by her mother's

---

[8] Ibid., p. 65.
[9] Ibid.
[10] Ibid., p. 67.

description of her as a "little devil" a few lines later. None-theless, the novel is not a formal allegory and, as such, the girl cannot be reduced to mere metaphor. As a real con-crete person, she transcends and supersedes such abstract personification. She may represent the sin on one level of meaning, but she is also the priest's real flesh-and-blood daughter, and, as such, her personhood demands our re-spect and our sympathy. It is precisely because she is a real person and not a mere personification that we find her behavior so alarming and, humanly speaking, improbable. We are similarly alarmed by the children who taunt Padre José so cruelly, and by the selfishly motivated children of the pious woman who are seemingly immune to the charms of the saccharined hagiographies that she reads to them.

Why is it that Greene is so seemingly allergic to the pres-ence of purity and sanctity in his work that he will not admit even a modicum of childlike innocence amid the gloom of human degradation? Returning to our initial assertion that Greene obsessively transposes a darker side onto all of his characters, so that even their goodness is warped, we lament his apparent unwillingness or inability to allow even the children their innocence. Contrary to Christ's exhor-tation that we must become like little children in order to enter the kingdom of heaven, Greene banishes any sense of heaven by refusing to admit the childlike into his fictional kingdom. Nobody is childlike in Greene's novels, not even the children themselves. Can anyone truly come to Christ in such dismal dystopias?

The same seeming allergy is reflected in Greene's un-willingness to admit the possibility of pure self-sacrificial motives for a man's calling to the priesthood, or at least an unwillingness to admit such self-sacrificial men into the subcreated world of his novels. We are told, with a crassness that seems to preclude the presence of grace, that the whisky priest "had believed that when he was a priest he would be rich and proud—that was called having a vocation".[11] This vacuous inability to discern the difference between a vocation and a vacation is hardly edifying, increasing the reader's creeping suspicion that edification is not high on Greene's list of artistic priorities. Similarly, the unwillingness of the Catholic peasants to betray the whisky priest to the authorities, even if it means laying down their own lives or the lives of their loved ones, cannot be depicted by Greene as motivated by a self-sacrificial love for God or the priest. On the contrary, the priest is "the trouble-maker who for obscure and superstitious reasons they preferred not to betray to the police".[12] In removing any trace of heroism or sanctity from their actions, Greene pushes credulity to breaking point and beyond. Nor can the priest be allowed a sense of gratitude toward those who have saved his life. On the contrary, he resents having been left with a "burden of gratitude to carry round with him".[13] Such is the underlying perversity that even thanksgiving itself is something for which we are not to be thankful!

In the midst of this spiritual miasma, we are not surprised to find the whisky priest offering his soul to the devil in return for the salvation of his child. He does so in a prayer to God, but even a rudimentary grasp of theology would have taught the priest that such a prayer was satanic. *"O God, give me any kind of death—without contrition, in a state of sin—only save this child. . . . I would give my life, that's nothing, my soul."*[14] To be fair to Greene, he does not seem

---

[11] Ibid.
[12] Ibid., p. 80.
[13] Ibid.
[14] Ibid., p. 82.

to endorse such a prayer, a fact to which the metaphorical symbolism of the appearance of "a tiny green snake" immediately after these attempts "to bribe God" attests,[15] but the lascivious pleasure with which he seems to place the prayer onto the lips of the priest is itself unhealthy.

The irony is that Greene's impious iconoclasm, his refusal to admit purity and sanctity into his fictional world, is less realistic than the pious iconography and hagiography that he mocks in the novel. The clumsily pious hagiographies that the devout woman reads to her children at the beginning and end of the novel may sin on the side of sweetness, adding unnecessary sugar to the truth, but Greene's exorcism of all life, all sweetness, and all hope from his novel is a denial of reality itself. It is not an embellishment of the truth but an abolition of it. And this irony has ironic ramifications. The ultimate irony is that Greene would have been incapable of writing the sequel to *The Power and the Glory* that his climax sets up. If the new priest who arrives to take the whisky priest's place had been a real saint, Greene would not have been able to write about him. Saints are beyond his creative reach, not because they are unreal or unreachable but because they are more real than the rest of us. Saints are more elusive than sinners because they are more real than sinners. They walk in the light, in the presence of Reality, while we lurk in the murk, and loiter in the shadows of our own *schadenfreude*.

And so we have sat in judgment of the whisky priest, and by implication of Greene also, mindful that we, too, must be judged. This being so, let's not be too harsh on these miserable sinners. There is much that passes for good, solid orthodoxy in the work, and much that is masterful in the art of storytelling and the use of metaphor. Take,

[15] Ibid., p. 83.

for instance, the lieutenant, the whisky priest's nemesis, antithesis, and alter ego. He is a priest of atheism: "There was something of a priest in his intent observant walk—a theologian going back over the errors of the past to destroy them again."[16] He is an iconoclast who ironically erects new icons to replace the old, replacing the devotional pictures of the Virgin and saints, with which the peasants adorned their walls, with a picture of the president of the Marxist Republic. "There was a picture of the President on the wall. . . . In the light of a candle [the room] looked as comfortless as a prison or a monastic cell."[17] To the lieutenant, the prison cell and the monastic cell are synonymous, and we find him, this priest of atheism, this monk of Marxism, alone in his cell, "infuriated . . . that there were still people in the state who believed in a loving and merciful God".[18] He, on the other hand, was "a mystic" who had "a complete certainty in the existence of a dying, cooling world of human beings who had evolved from animals for no purpose at all".[19] As ever, Greene's narrative drips with provocative irony. Although Greene, in his darker Mr. Hyde persona, is alarmingly and disarmingly convincing as the devil's advocate, he can also mock the devil's disciples by hinting that a belief in a Godless cosmos is itself singularly "mystical". The implicit and underlying irony is that an atheist must make a leap of faith in nothing as much as the theist makes a leap of faith in something. It takes faith to believe in God, but it also takes faith not to believe in Him. And thus, Greene shows us one of the great jokes at the very heart of the human condition. Faith

[16] Ibid., p. 24.
[17] Ibid.
[18] Ibid.
[19] Ibid., pp. 24–25.

is essentially unavoidable. Even atheists cannot avoid acting on faith.

Let's end, therefore, with a genuine act of faith on the
part of the whisky priest, a prayer that is answered at the
novel's end: "O God, forgive me—I am a proud, lust-
ful, greedy man. I have loved authority too much. These
people are martyrs—protecting me with their own lives.
They deserve a martyr to care for them—not a man like
me, who loves all the wrong things. Perhaps I had better
escape—if I tell people how it is over here, perhaps they
will send a good man with a fire of love."[20]

[20] Ibid., pp. 95–96.

Chapter Twelve

Brideshead Revisited

It seems to me that in the present phase of European history the essential issue is no longer between Catholicism, on one side, and Protestantism, on the other, but between Christianity and Chaos.

—Evelyn Waugh

These fighting words by the novelist Evelyn Waugh are from a full-page, banner-headlined article that followed two leading articles in the *Daily Express*, discussing the significance of his recent reception into the Catholic Church. The article continues,

Today we can see it on all sides as the active negation of all that western culture has stood for. Civilization—and by this I do not mean talking cinemas and tinned food, nor even surgery and hygienic houses, but the whole moral and artistic organization of Europe—has not in itself the power of survival. It came into being through Christianity, and without it has no significance or power to command allegiance. The loss of faith in Christianity and the consequential lack of confidence in moral and social

Evelyn Waugh, "Converted to Rome: Why It Has Happened to Me", *Daily Express*, October 1930.

standards have become embodied in the ideal of a materialistic, mechanized state.... It is no longer possible ... to accept the benefits of civilization and at the same time deny the supernatural basis upon which it rests.

On the day after the publication of Waugh's article, Edward Rosslyn Mitchell, a Protestant Member of Parliament, wrote a reply or riposte; on the following day, Fr. Woodlock, a Jesuit, wrote an article entitled "Is Britain Turning to Rome?" Three days later, an entire page was given over to the ensuing letters.

Seldom had a religious conversion caused such controversy. Back in 1845, John Henry Newman's conversion had rocked the establishment, as had the conversion in 1903 of Robert Hugh Benson, son of the Archbishop of Canterbury, and the conversion in 1917 of Ronald Knox, son of the Bishop of Manchester. Yet the consternation over Waugh's conversion was different. Whereas these earlier controversial conversions had been connected to the defection of clergymen from one church to another, Waugh was regarded as a typical hedonistic modern youth who was presumed to have had an iconoclastic disdain for all religion. As such, his conversion was greeted with utter astonishment by the media and the literary establishment. On the morning after his reception into the Church, the leading article in the *Daily Express* expressed bemused bewilderment that an author notorious for his "almost passionate adherence to the ultra-modern" could have become a Catholic.

Waugh's newfound Christian faith found expression in the novels published in the years following his conversion, especially in *A Handful of Dust*, which took its title from a line in "The Waste Land" by T. S. Eliot, whose own conversion to Anglo-Catholicism in 1928 had also baffled the *literati* and the secular media. It was, however, *Brideshead Revisited*, the novel that Waugh considered his magnum opus, that most successfully embodies the tension between Waugh's ultramontane faith and the ultramodern world in which it found itself.

Published in 1945, *Brideshead Revisited* traces the interaction between Charles Ryder, its ostensibly agnostic narrator, and a family of aristocratic Catholics. In the Preface to the second edition, Waugh wrote that its theme was "the operation of divine grace on a group of diverse but closely connected characters". This authorial and therefore authoritative exposition of the theme is key, in the literal sense that it unlocks the deepest levels of meaning in the work. If the key theme is the operation of divine grace, it means that there is a hidden hand at work, a supernatural presence operating on the characters. It's as though the novel's chief protagonist is not any of the visible characters but is God Himself, whose omnipotent and omniscient presence guides the narrative. From a Christian perspective, this is nothing less than realism, in the sense that it reflects reality. It is, however, very difficult for a novelist to suggest this presence without descending to the level of didacticism and preachiness, two traits that are usually destructive to the power of the Muse. It is, therefore, a mark of Waugh's brilliance that he succeeds with a theme that he himself described as "perhaps presumptuously large".

Although the author's epigraphic note ("I am not I: thou art not he or she: they are not they") signifies the author's desire to distance himself and his readers from any of the characters, it is evident that there is much of Waugh's own preconversion self in the characterization of Charles Ryder, the agnostic narrator through whom we see the story unfold. And yet, with a stroke of subtle brilliance, Waugh subverts the agnosticism of the narrative voice through its being spoken by the older Ryder, recalling the events of his life from a mature middle age, at which point, as we discover in the Epilogue, he has himself embraced the faith. Thus, the narrator expresses the religious doubts of his youth from the perspective of one who now doubts those doubts. In this sense, it is hard to see Ryder without seeing a shadow of Waugh, musing upon his own loss of faith as a youth and his years as a hedonistic agnostic at Oxford. Thus, for instance, Ryder's account of the disastrous effects of theological modernism on his own faith as a schoolboy reflects those of Waugh's experience at Lancing College. Similarly, Ryder's account of undergraduate decadence and debauchery reflects Waugh's own riotous hedonism at Oxford.

The menagerie of characters that breathe life into the novel are drawn with Dickensian dexterity, and, on occasion, with Dickensian grotesqueness, suggestive of caricature, as is the case with the effete mannerisms of Anthony Blanche, the sordid creepiness of Mr. Samgrass, and the sadistic humor of Charles' father, the last of whom was played to hilarious perfection by Sir John Gielgud in the British television adaptation of the 1980s. As for the Catholic aristocratic family with whom Ryder interacts, they are some of the most memorable characters in modern fiction: Lord Marchmain, who deserts his wife and family and takes up with a concubine in Venice, is "conscious of a Byronic aura, which he considered to be in bad taste and was at pains to suppress"[1]; Lady Marchmain, the deserted wife and mother, is pious in her faith but unable to win the affection of her children; Lord Brideshead, the eldest of the children and heir to the estate, is Jesuit-educated, deeply pious but socially inept; Sebastian, Eton-educated and therefore

---

[1] Evelyn Waugh, *Brideshead Revisited* (New York: Little, Brown, 1999), p. 97.

ill-equipped to grasp the rational underpinnings of faith, is self-consciously self-centered and lacking the desire or ability to grow up and grasp the responsibilities of adulthood; Julia, the older of the two daughters, is as self-centered as her brother, though less consciously, and shares his resentment of the way in which Catholicism is an obstacle to self-gratification; and, last but indubitably not least, Cordelia, the youngest of the family, is pious and precocious in equal measure and reminds us, as Waugh clearly intends, of her famous Shakespearean namesake.

The dynamic of the plot flows in two directions. In the first half of the novel, Sebastian and Julia stray further and further from their mother's reach and further from the faith with which they associate her. Sebastian descends into alcoholism and social dereliction, living a life of increased squalor in North Africa, whereas Julia makes a reckless and ultimately disastrous marriage to a cynical and ambitious politician and later begins an adulterous relationship with Ryder. After Julia had "shut her mind against her religion",[2] we are told of the suffering that her children's apostasy is causing Lady Marchmain:

> And Lady Marchmain saw this and added it to her new grief for Sebastian and her old grief for her husband and to the deadly sickness in her body, and took all these sorrows with her daily to church; it seemed her heart was transfixed with the swords of her dolours, a living heart to match the plaster and paint; what comfort she took home with her, God knows.[3]

It is after Lady Marchmain's death that the tide begins to turn or, to employ the metaphor that Waugh borrows

[2] Ibid., p. 189.
[3] Ibid.

from G. K. Chesterton, it is after her death that there is the "twitch upon the thread" that begins to tug the prodigals back. This image or metaphor for grace is mentioned by Cordelia as she contemplates the way in which her father had left both his wife and the faith to which he had converted upon marrying her:

> Anyhow, the family haven't been very constant, have they? There's him gone and Sebastian gone and Julia gone. But God won't let them go for long, you know. I wonder if you remember the story mummy read us the evening Sebastian first got drunk—I mean the *bad* evening. "Father Brown" said something like "I caught him" (the thief) "with an unseen hook and an invisible line which is long enough to let him wander to the ends of the world and still bring him back with a twitch upon the thread."[4]

From a worldly perspective, it is easy to find in Lady Marchmain a convenient scapegoat whose relentless adherence to the faith has alienated her husband and children (or two of them at least) from herself and her religion. This is indeed the way that the novel is often read and taught in our meretricious age, which explains why the director of the recent and lamentably bad Hollywood adaptation of the novel proclaimed that, in his version (or spin), God was the enemy.

If, however, we take Waugh at his word and expect to find the operation of divine grace at work in the story, we need to seek the supernatural dimension. If we see with these theologically attuned eyes, we realize that Lady Marchmain's influence on her husband and children does not cease upon her death. Apart from the power that the memory of her invokes, there is the very real power of

---

[4] *Brideshead Revisited*, p. 220.

her prayers, both before and after her death. Her ghost continues to haunt her family, in the benign sense that she intercedes for them. Furthermore, it seems that her intercessory prayers are answered in dramatic fashion as Lord Marchmain, Julia, and Sebastian return to the fold.

And yet in each case, the conversion of heart does not come without a great deal of suffering. "No one is ever holy without suffering,"[5] says Cordelia, and it's no surprise that the other powerful metaphor for grace that Waugh employs as the novel reaches its climax is that of an avalanche that destroys everything in its path:

> And another image came to me, of an arctic hut and a trapper alone with his furs and oil lamp and log fire; everything dry and ship-shape and warm inside, and outside the last blizzard of winter raging and the snow piling up against the door. Quite silently a great weight forming against the timber; the bolt straining in its socket; minute by minute in the darkness outside the white heap sealing the door, until quite when the wind dropped and the sun came out on the ice slopes and the thaw set in a block would move, slide, and tumble, high above, gather weight, till the whole hillside seemed to be falling, and the little lighted place would open and splinter and disappear, rolling with the avalanche into the ravine.[6]

The trapper is Charles Ryder, whose little world of comfort, planned with his future marriage to Julia in mind, is about to be swept away. Thus, as Julia decides that her dying father should see a priest, Charles has "the sense that the fate of more souls than one was at issue; that the snow was beginning to shift on the high slopes".[7] A little later,

---

[5] Ibid., p. 309.
[6] Ibid., pp. 310–11.
[7] Ibid., p. 326.

his worst fears are realized as Julia breaks off their engagement: "I can't marry you, Charles; I can't be with you
ever again.... I've always been bad. Probably I shall be bad
again, punished again. But the worse I am, the more I need
God. I can't shut myself out from his mercy. That is what it
would mean; starting a life with you, without him."[8]

The final words of the final chapter are a reprise of the
metaphor: "The avalanche was down, the hillside swept
bare behind it; the last echoes died on the white slopes;
the new mound glittered and lay still in the silent val-
ley."[9] The final chapter ends, therefore, with Ryder's life
in ruins, swept away in the avalanche of grace that had
brought Julia and her father back to the faith. And yet,
like every good Christian story, there is life after death, or,
perhaps we should say, there is a resurrection.

Earlier in the novel, Charles had turned his back on
Brideshead, the ancestral home of the Flyte family, the
name of which is symbolic of the Church herself, the Bride
of Christ, whose "head" is Christ, the Bridegroom:

> But as I drove away and turned back in the car to take
> what promised to be my last view of the house, I felt that
> I was leaving part of myself behind, and that wherever I
> went afterwards I should feel the lack of it, and search for
> it hopelessly, as ghosts are said to do, frequenting the spots
> where they buried material treasures without which they
> cannot pay their way to the nether world....
>
> "I have left behind illusion," I said to myself. "Hence-
> forth I live in a world of three dimensions—with the aid
> of my five senses."
>
> I have since learned that there is no such world.[10]

[8] Ibid., p. 340.
[9] Ibid., p. 341.
[10] Ibid., p. 169.

Here we see the subversive voice of the older Charles rebuking his younger self for his naïve atheism. And it is this older Charles whom we meet in the novel's Epilogue. Returning to Brideshead several years after the cataclysmic death of all his hopes at the end of the final chapter, he kneels and prays before the tabernacle in the chapel. Like Julia, who is now symbolically in the Holy Land with Brideshead and Cordelia, he has embraced the ancient faith. Now, at last, Charles can speak with the same voice as Waugh, who wrote of his own conversion that it was "like stepping across the chimney piece out of a Looking-Glass world, where everything is an absurd caricature, into the real world God made; and then begins the delicious process of exploring it limitlessly".[11] It is no wonder that we are told at the novel's conclusion that Charles was "looking unusually cheerful today".[12]

[11] Quoted in Michael de-la-Noy, *Eddy: The Life of Edward Sackville-West* (London: Bodley Head, 1988), pp. 237–38.

[12] *Brideshead Revisited*, p. 351.

APPENDIX

The Mystery of *Sir Thomas More*

The late Elizabethan or early Jacobean play *Sir Thomas More* is one of the most intriguing, fascinating, and mysterious works of literature ever written. Its importance is not connected primarily to its literary merit, though it represents a fine if flawed example of early modern English dramaturgy, but in its historical importance. A pro-Catholic play written in very anti-Catholic times, it offers valuable insights into the nature of state censorship in late sixteenth-century and early seventeenth-century England and illustrates the powerful presence of Sir Thomas More in England's cultural, religious, and political consciousness more than sixty years after his martyrdom. Most important is its connection to William Shakespeare and the evidence it offers for Shakespeare's Catholic sympathies.

The study of the original manuscript of *Sir Thomas More* has preoccupied many of the finest historians and literary critics and has served to highlight the power and the prejudice of literary scholarship. On the one hand, there seems to be a consensus with regard to the identity of the various writers whose handwriting appears on the manuscript, yet, on the other, there is anything but a consensus with regard to the relationship of these writers with one another and with the work as a whole. Most controversial is the extent and the nature of Shakespeare's involvement with the play and its importance to our understanding of Shakespeare's own philosophical, theological, and political beliefs. In short and in sum, *Sir Thomas More* is more than simply a play; it is a mystery, the unraveling of which is important to our understanding of the world's greatest playwright and the nature of the times in which he lived.

The original manuscript of the play, which contains the handwriting of seven different people and is kept in the Harleian collection at the British Museum in London, has a fascinating history. Its earliest known owner was John Murray, an eighteenth-century collector of rare books and manuscripts. The manuscript was first published in 1844 by the Shakespeare Society, edited by the literary historian Alexander Dyce. Shakespeare's involvement in the writing of the play was first suggested by the pioneering scholar Richard Simpson in 1871, a view that was accepted, with reservation, by James Spedding, editor of the works of Sir Francis Bacon, a year later. In 1911, the manuscript was reproduced in typographical facsimile, edited by W. W. Greg, in a work that the *Reader's Encyclopedia of Shakespeare* described as "one of the finest examples of English literary scholarship".[1] Five years later, the palaeographer Sir Edward Maunde Thompson published a meticulously detailed study of the handwriting of one of the contributors to the manuscript and declared that it was the work of Shakespeare. In 1923, Greg and Thompson joined forces with three other preeminent Shakespeare scholars, A. W. Pollard, J. Dover Wilson, and R. W. Chambers, to publish *Shakespeare's Hand in the Play of Sir Thomas More*,[2] which established

---

[1] Oscar James Campbell and Edward G. Quinn, eds., *The Reader's Encyclopedia of Shakespeare* (New York: MJF Books, 1966), p. 799.

[2] Alfred W. Pollard et al., *Shakespeare's Hand in the Play of Sir Thomas More* (Cambridge: Cambridge University Press, 1923).

authoritatively Shakespeare's involvement in the writing of the play. Today, authoritative editions of Shakespeare's works, such as the Oxford Shakespeare and the Arden Shakespeare, include *Sir Thomas More* as part of the Shakespearean canon. In 2005, more than four hundred years after its original composition, the play was finally performed by the Royal Shakespeare Company.

Apart from Shakespeare, the manuscript contains the handwriting of six other people. The bulk of the manuscript, known to scholars as Hand S, was written or transcribed by Anthony Munday, with additional passages written by Henry Chettle (Hand A), Thomas Heywood (Hand B), an anonymous scribe (Hand C), William Shakespeare (H and D), and Thomas Dekker (Hand E). The seventh and final handwriting to appear on the manuscript is that of Sir Edmund Tilney, the Master of the Revels, the Elizabethan and Jacobean state's official censor. Rather beguilingly, therefore, *Sir Thomas More* shows a level of collaboration between five of the best-known dramatists of the period and also the words of direct censorship by the representative of the state.

If, as an historical document, the manuscript of the play is priceless, it is also explosive, causing a great deal of division and debate among historians and literary critics. Disagreement has emerged with regard to the dating of the original manuscript, written or transcribed by Munday, and the time that elapsed before the four other playwrights and the anonymous scribe became involved. Although it is generally agreed that the unusual collaboration between rival dramatists with very disparate views was instigated with the apparent purpose of placating Tilney so that the play could be published and performed, there is no consensus as to why Protestant and Catholic writers should unite to circumvent the censorship of an obviously and avowedly pro-Catholic play. Why would Munday, who had a reputation for being virulently anti-Catholic, have written a play in which the Catholic martyr, Thomas More, is the undoubted hero? Might the apparent incongruity of such a scenario suggest that Munday was not the principal author but had been merely the transcriber of a play written by someone else? Might the original author of much of the play be none other than Shakespeare himself? Might he have written much more than the relatively short passage written in his own hand that critical consensus has ascribed to him? Yet if Munday was not the play's principal author, why would he consent to transcribe the play on the author's behalf? Such questions shroud *Sir Thomas More* in mystery, bestowing upon it a mystique that is both attractive to the scholar but also perilous to his reputation.

In order to understand better the various arguments that surround the dating and the authorship of the play, it is necessary to be conversant with the manuscript itself. On its very first page, in the margin to the left of the opening lines of the original text written or transcribed by Anthony Munday, are the words of Sir Edmund Tilney, the state censor, who was Master of the Revels from 1579 until his death in 1610. Tilney instructs Munday to "leave out the insurrection wholly and the cause thereof, and begin with Sir Thomas More at the Mayor's sessions, with a report of his good service done being Sheriff of London upon a mutiny against the Lombards—only by a short report, and not otherwise, at your own perils."[3] The fact that Tilney's words are addressed to more than one person might suggest his knowledge of the collaborative nature

---

[3] Handwritten notes in original manuscript of Anthony Munday, *The book of Sir Thomas More*, British Museum, Harleian collection.

of the authorship of the original text, of which Munday may have been simply the transcriber or perhaps one of the several authors involved. On the other hand, Tilney's comments appear only on Munday's original text and not on the various insertions in the hands of the other playwrights, suggesting that these were appended after Tilney's original censorship. It is, however, possible that the other dramatists (Shakespeare, Chettle, Dekker, and Heywood) were involved as coauthors and that Tilney's words are addressed to the collective group. Let's not forget that Tilney would have been sent a "clean" final version of the play, transcribed neatly in a single hand, and would not have received earlier drafts on which the various handwriting would have appeared. In short, the fact that the original text censored by Tilney was written solely in the hand of a solitary scribe, Anthony Munday, does not prove that Munday was the sole author of the play. Indeed, the fact that Tilney is clearly addressing his concerns to a group of people might suggest otherwise. A more prosaic interpretation might conclude that Tilney is addressing the playing company and not merely the author. In any event, the fact remains that Munday's transcription of the clean version of the play does not necessarily denote his sole authorship of the original text. This being so, it is possible that at least some of the other writers were involved in the writing of the original text, which would help to explain their evident involvement in the efforts to circumvent Tilney's censorship. As stakeholders in the original manuscript, they would have a vested interest in seeing its being approved for performance and publication.

The fact that Tilney's initial concern was the excision of the whole insurrection scene has led, reasonably enough, to the assumption that he was concerned primarily with the danger to public order, believing that the play could inflame the anti-immigrant sentiments of Londoners. Although the so-called Ill May Day insurrection of 1517, the subject of the scene that Tilney insisted be removed, had happened almost a century earlier, anti-immigrant sentiment remained widespread among Londoners and tensions remained high. The Shakespeare scholar A. W. Pollard detailed anti-alien disturbances in London in 1586, 1593, and 1595, conjecturing that *Sir Thomas More* might have been written in the period of these latter-day riots, thereby explaining Tilney's sensitivity to the presentation of anti-immigrant riots on the stage. Although, as we shall see, it is extremely unlikely that the play would have been sent to Tilney until 1603, tensions between Londoners and immigrants were still running high in the early seventeenth century, and the danger of new anti-immigrant riots would no doubt have been on Tilney's mind.

Unfortunately, Tilney's first act of censorship has often been allowed to eclipse the censorship that follows it. He was also at pains to remove or minimize any suggestion that Sir Thomas More and his fellow martyr, John Fisher, Bishop of Rochester, were justified in their refusal to kowtow to Henry VIII's demands that they sign the Oath of Supremacy, thereby recognizing the king as supreme head of the Church in England. Tilney deleted the whole of the passage in which More and Fisher, later to be canonized by the Catholic Church as martyrs, are shown to be right and virtuous in their opposition to the king's imposition of a state religion. Tilney's unease at such praise of Catholic dissidents in the heated religious and political situation in Elizabethan and Jacobean England is hardly surprising. Indeed, one wonders why the playwrights should have believed that such overt criticism of Queen Elizabeth's father and such obvious sympathy for Catholic martyrs would ever escape the censorship of the ever vigilant Tilney. Quite simply, Thomas More was still a hot potato, more than sixty years after his death, touching a raw nerve, not only with Elizabeth, whose father had the saint's blood on his hands, but with the Elizabethan state as a whole. Thomas More had been executed by the reigning monarch for refusing to compromise his Catholic conscience on the altar of Machiavellian *realpolitik*, making him an archetype for the English Martyrs who had suffered a similar fate in the reign of Elizabeth. As such, any positive depiction of More could be seen as a dangerous indictment of England's present rulers. Considering that Catholic priests were being put to death in the 1590s and considering that Elizabeth was a jealous guardian of her position as head of the Church of England, inherited from her father, it was surely unthinkable that such a play would ever be approved in Elizabeth's reign.

Such evidence points inescapably to the play being submitted to Tilney after Elizabeth's death in March 1603, at a time when it was widely believed that the new king, James I, would show tolerance to Catholicism, as he had hinted in the years before his accession and as was suggested by the fact that his wife was known to be a Catholic. It was seen as confirmation of James' moderation in religious matters that one of his first acts following his accession was to make peace with Spain, thereby significantly alleviating the religiously charged atmosphere of English foreign policy. In the first year of his reign, it was decreed that fines and other penalties would no longer be imposed on Catholics. With the onerous pecuniary burden removed, thousands of closet Catholics stayed away from Anglican services and sought once again to practice their faith fully and openly. "It was at once apparent," wrote Heinrich Mutschmann and Karl Wentersdorf, "that Elizabeth's policy of extermination had not achieved its purpose, and that

Catholicism still constituted a formidable power in most parts of the country."[4]

There is no doubt that England's beleaguered Catholic population felt a sense of elation that "Bloody Bess" had died, hoping that the decades of relentless persecution would die with her. Shakespeare's own sense of elation is perhaps evident in the title of the comedy *All's Well That Ends Well*, which he wrote at around this time, and also in the writing of *Measure for Measure*, arguably his most openly Catholic play. It's almost as though a huge weight had been lifted from the Bard's overburdened muse and that he felt finally able to express himself more freely without fear of censorship or retribution. If the evidence of these plays is to be believed, it is clear that the "honeymoon period" following James' accession presented a golden opportunity to publish a play on the martyr Sir Thomas More, which would have been impossible earlier.

The honeymoon period would be short-lived, lasting from the queen's death in March 1603 to the renewal of full-blown anti-Catholic persecution in July of the following year. It is extremely likely, therefore, that the play was submitted to Tilney during this sixteen-month period and that the revisions in the handwriting of the other playwrights were also written during this period. Following the renewal of persecution, all hopes of the play getting past the censor would have evaporated as would the unusual collaboration of the five playwrights.

Another question raised by the play's overt sympathy for Catholic martyrs is why Munday, who had been active in the anti-Catholic spy network and was directly or indirectly responsible for sending Catholic priests to

---

[4] H. Mutschmann and K. Wentersdorf, *Shakespeare and Catholicism* (New York: Sheed and Ward, 1952), pp. 27–28.

their deaths, should have written so sympathetically of his erstwhile enemies. In 1578, when still a teenager, he had been sent abroad to spy on the activities of English Catholic refugees. Feigning a desire to become a priest, he had gained admittance to the English College in Rome, where he gathered material for his exposé of the College and its activities that was published in 1582 as *The English Romayne Life*. In the previous year, he had been involved in the betrayal and capture of Edmund Campion. It is, therefore, a little puzzling that Munday, many years later, should choose Thomas More as his subject, and it is tempting to detect something of a change of heart on the playwright's part akin to that discernible in Marlowe's *Dr. Faustus*.

Understandably enough, some scholars have doubted that Munday could have been responsible for such a pro-Catholic play and have sought the true author among one or other of Munday's collaborators. Although such a conclusion seems reasonable enough, we still have to wonder why Munday, even if he was only the play's transcriber, should have had such an apparent change of heart. The Elizabethan scholar Muriel St. Clare Byrne clearly considered him as being almost psychopathic in his hatred of Catholicism:

> Munday *liked* seeing Jesuits hanged and then drawn and quartered; and Munday liked such a sight not because it was the heyday of the Renaissance and passions ran high, ... not because he lived in the spacious times of great Elizabeth, but because he was one of those human beings who find a ghastly and secret pleasure in seeing other people hurt.[5]

[5] Muriel St. Clare Byrne, unpublished work in progress at the time of her death, quoted in John Jowett, ed., *Sir Thomas More* (London: Arden Shakespeare, 2011), p. 12.

Is it possible that such a man could have written *Sir Thomas More*? Yet the fact remains that the bulk of the text of the play is evidently in Munday's handwriting. The answer to the riddle may be found in his notorious opportunism, which had been satirized by John Davies in 1594 in an epigram punning on Munday's name:

> Munday I sweare shalbee a hollidaye,
> If hee forsweare himself but once a daye.[6]

In the modern idiom, Davies' epigram is saying that it will be a month of Sundays before Munday can go a day without lying or perjuring himself. Could such a man have written so eloquently about two Catholics, Thomas More and John Fisher, who would prefer to be put to death rather than forswear themselves?

A further key to understanding the vacillations of Anthony Munday, whose theological and political affiliations seem to have changed with the changing religious and political climate of the day, is provided by the writer and literary scholar David Womersley, who goes to the disingenuous heart of Munday's religious posturing:

> Was it the case that, when in Rome, he played the part of a Catholic? Or was it rather that, when he returned to England, he played the part of a Protestant? Or do we not have to choose between these alternatives? Was religious affiliation for Munday in fact just another expression of the extemporizing theatrical talent he had displayed as a boy? Was he therefore always acting, always simply trying on different religious identities for size and, like a religious chameleon, hoping to blend in to the background?

[6] John Davies, *Poems*, ed. Robert Krueger (Oxford: Clarendon Press, 1975), p. 157.

Certainly, it is hard to pick out any thread of consistency running through Munday's religious activities and associations. This sometime scholar of the English College in Rome on his return to London became a friend of the ferocious Protestant and Marian exile, Robert Crowley. Later still he befriended and worked with the crypto-Catholic antiquarian and historian John Stow. By all accounts an officious and even overly-energetic hunter-out of recusants, Munday was just as happy, a few years later, to be equally busy (although less successful) in attempts to suppress the anti-episcopal writings of Martin Marprelate.[7]

On the one hand, Munday had betrayed Catholic recusants—that is, dissidents—to their deaths and, on the other, had also betrayed Puritan and Calvinist nonconformists who wrote "anti-episcopal" attacks on the Church of England. At this juncture, we might be tempted to understand Munday's actions on the basis of his desire to defend the established church—that is, the Anglican episcopacy—from its enemies on both the Catholic and the Protestant ends of the religious spectrum. And yet he was not trusted by the Anglicans either. A pamphlet published in 1589 imagines John Whitgift, the Archbishop of Canterbury, condemning Munday for betraying the Anglican church: "Ah, thou Judas, thou that has already betrayed the Papists, I think meanest to betray us also."[8] Munday was trusted by nobody and was considered to be a Judas by everybody!

Having analyzed Munday's unprincipled opportunism, it seems likely that his eagerness to be involved in the writing or transcription of *Sir Thomas More* was an attempt to ingratiate himself with what he perceived as

[7] Quoted in Jowett, *Sir Thomas More*, p. 13.

[8] Quoted in Donna B. Hamilton, *Anthony Munday and the Catholics, 1560–1633* (Aldershot: Ashgate, 2005), p. 65.

the Catholic ascendency on the accession of James to the throne. Wishing to back what he thought might be the winning side, and wishing to be seen to be atoning for his past sins against the papists, he was at pains to show his Catholic sympathies in the new order heralded by the new king. The fact that Munday quickly reverted to his anti-papist position following the resumption of anti-Catholic persecution reinforces the suspicion that his involvement in the play was an act of self-serving cynicism.

Why, one wonders, should the other collaborators, especially the pro-Catholic Shakespeare, have sought or tolerated Munday's involvement? None of them would have been naïve enough to trust him or to feel that his "conversion" to the cause of More and Fisher was genuine. Perhaps he was chosen to transcribe the play precisely because of his anti-Catholic track record and because he was known by Tilney to have always served the interests of the state against its nonconformist dissidents, both Catholic and Puritan. Munday might have been selected as the nonpartisan front man in the efforts of Shakespeare and others to navigate *Sir Thomas More* through the perilous waters of state censorship.

There is an intriguing postscript to the life of Anthony Munday, which might throw some additional light on his motives for writing or transcribing the play. The poet John Taylor, writing in 1638, five years after Munday's death, suggests that Munday paid a high psychological price for his involvement in hounding Catholic priests to their deaths. Taylor reported that, in old age, Munday "would run from the Table at the sight of a forequarter of Lambe roasted",[9] which John Jowett concludes was "a neurotic

---

[9] John Taylor, from *Taylor's Feast* (1638), quoted in Jowett, *Sir Thomas More*, p. 15.

aversion that might relate to his early involvement in the reduction of human beings to butchered carcasses".[10] Jowett, a firm believer that Munday was the principal author of the play, conjectures that "part of the genesis of *Sir Thomas More* lay in its vacillating main author's need for atonement."[11] Although it is possible that Munday may have written the play in an effort to ingratiate himself with what he perceived as the new Catholic ascendency, it is more difficult to believe that a desire for atonement was a major motivation considering his instant reversion to his old papist-baiting ways once he realized that Catholics were once again *personae non gratae*. *Pace* Jowett, it would seem more likely that Munday was merely the transcriber of the play, who may or may not have had a minor role in the writing of it. If this is so, the play's authorship is thrown into question.

Since Chettle, Dekker, and Heywood were all, to one degree or another, antagonistic toward Catholicism, the possibility of Shakespeare's authorship of the play comes to the fore. The literary historian and critic Thomas Merriam has made a meticulously researched case for Shakespeare's authorship, employing stylometry to show that *Sir Thomas More* has more stylistic qualities in common with Shakespeare's plays than with the works of Munday. This being so, let's turn our attention to Shakespeare.

A closer perusal of Shakespeare's undisputed contribution to the play, the section written in his own handwriting, will illustrate his sympathy with More and the presence of the lessons to be learned by his own time from More's holy example. The lines attributed to Shakespeare depict Thomas More's efforts to reason with a riotous mob

---

[10] Jowett, *Sir Thomas More*, p. 15.
[11] Ibid.

intent on attacking recently arrived immigrants who are perceived as threatening the livelihoods of the indigenous population. His counsel of Christian charity calms the storm of rebellion. The crowd is appeased and declares, in unison, that he "says true" and that, as good Christians echoing the words of the Gospel, they should "do as we may be done by". More's words in the play resonate with those of Menenius Agrippa to the restive plebeians in *Coriolanus* and with those of Portia to the vengeful Shylock in *The Merchant of Venice*. Such words, placed in the mouth of a Catholic martyr who was beheaded by a merciless king, have particular power and resonate with the last words of another martyr, Robert Southwell, who was hanged, drawn, and quartered in 1595 by a merciless queen. Southwell's last words are taken from Scripture, and it is possible that Shakespeare, who almost certainly knew Southwell well and who may have been present when Southwell uttered them from the scaffold, had these words from Scripture in mind as he placed a commentary upon them into the mouth of More:

> But thou, why judgest thou thy brother? Or thou, why dost thou despise thy brother? For we shall all stand before the judgment seat of Christ.... Let us not, therefore, judge one another any more. But judge this rather, that you put not a stumbling-block or a scandal in your brother's way.... Therefore let us follow after the things that are of peace, and keep the things that are of edification, one towards another.[12]

Even more intriguing than the 149 lines believed to be in Shakespeare's own hand are the twenty-one lines later

---

[12] These lines from Romans 14:10, 13, 19 were recited by Robert Southwell from the scaffold on the day of his execution.

in the play, written in the hand of an anonymous scribe but ascribed by critical consensus to Shakespeare. These are the words that Shakespeare puts in the mouth of Sir Thomas More, immediately after his appointment as the new Lord Chancellor, as he contemplates the responsibilities of his political office:

> It is in heaven that I am thus and thus,
> And that which we profanely term our fortunes
> Is the provision of the power above,
> Fitted and shap'd just to that strength of nature
> Which we are born [withal]. Good God, good God
> That I from such an humble bench of birth
> Should step, as 'twere up to my country's head
> And give the law out there. I in my father's life
> To take prerogative and tithe of knees
> From elder kinsmen, and him bind by my place
> To give the smooth and dexter way to me
> That owe it him by nature. Sure these things
> Not physick'd by respect might turn our blood
> To much corruption. But, More, the more thou hast
> Either of honor, office, wealth, and calling,
> Which might accite thee to embrace and hug them,
> The more do thou in serpents' natures think them,
> Fear their gay skins with thought of their sharp state,
> And let this be thy maxime: to be great
> Is, when the thread of hazard is once spun,
> A bottom great wound up, greatly undone.

According to Fernando de Mello Moser, a scholar of both More and Shakespeare, this soliloquy represents "a perfectly clear presentation of the awareness of two planes of existence: that of the provision of the power above, which we profanely call fortunes, and that of human vanities, wearing gay serpent skins but, like serpents, only too likely to bite mortally, through the temptation of worldly advantage turning these into an end in themselves, and thereby ultimately destroying the victim on both planes of existence at the same time.... Thomas More had chosen to fall—at one level, certainly, for the sake of the higher one."[13] Interestingly, Moser also connects the underlying and underpinning philosophy of this soliloquy with both the medieval past and the Baroque future, stressing the Catholicism inherent in both: "As I see it, the speech presents an example of the ... subordination of the Wheel of Fortune, in the religious sphere, to the workings of Providence: an achievement of the late medieval tradition which reappears, modified, in the Jesuit drama of the Baroque Age."[14] In essence, we see much of Shakespeare's own Catholic philosophy encapsulated within these few lines. Reality is to be understood in the profundity of providence not in the profanity of worldly fortune. So axiomatic is this understanding of reality that it is the motive force and the leitmotif of much of Shakespeare's work. On the one hand, we have the heroes and heroines of his plays, pursuing virtue and embracing suffering, and on the other, we have the Machiavels, pursuing self-interest and inflicting suffering on others. This being so, it is difficult indeed to read the plays without being reminded of the likes of Thomas More and Robert Southwell, on the one hand, and Henry VIII and Elizabeth on the other.

Further evidence of Shakespeare's admiration for More is discernible in Shakespeare's Sonnet 23, in which we see the same pun on More's name that he used in the lines cited above:

[13] Fernando de Mello Moser, *Dilecta Britannia: Estudos de Cultura Inglesa* (Lisbon, Portugal: Fundação Calouste Gulbenkian, 2004), pp. 150–51.

[14] Ibid., p. 150.

As an unperfect actor on the stage,
Who with his fear is put besides his part,
Or some fierce thing replete with too much rage,
Whose strength's abundance weakens his own heart;
So I for fear of trust forget to say
The perfect ceremony of love's right,
And in mine own love's strength seem to decay,
O'ercharged with burden of mine own love's might:
O let my books be then the eloquence,
And dumb presagers of my speaking breast,
Who plead for love, and look for recompense,
More than that love which more hath more expressed.
O learn to read what silent love hath writ,
To hear with eyes belongs to love's fine wit.

Clearly, the twelfth line of the sonnet comes alive with allegorical significance when the middle "more" is capitalized: "More than that love which [M]ore hath more expressed." Once the pun is accepted, the sonnet springs to life metaphysically, contrasting Shakespeare's own "unperfect" love, weakened by "fear" and "rage", with the holy love "which [M]ore hath more expressed". There is also a sublime allusion to the Mass as "the perfect ceremony of love's right", reinforced by the pun on "right/rite", and illustrating a deep theological understanding of the Mass as the "perfect ceremony" that re-presents Christ's death for sinners as "love's right" and "love's rite". Unlocking this beguiling sonnet still further we see that the poet laments that he is not present at this "perfect ceremony" as often as he should be because of "fear of trust", perhaps a reference to the spies who were present at these secret Masses intent on reporting the names of "papists" and on betraying the priests to the authorities. Since he does not have the heroic self-sacrificial love, even unto death, of a Thomas More (or a Robert Southwell), the poet desires that his "books" be his "eloquence", the "dumb presagers of my speaking breast". The final two lines are surely addressed both to the poet himself and to his reader, beseeching the latter to "learn to read" in his plays what the poet's love, silent through fear, dare not speak openly. Since they will not *hear* the poet speak his mind openly, his readers must *see* what he means in his plays, hearing with their eyes and using their own "love's fine wit" to discern his deeper meaning.

> O learn to read what silent love hath writ,
> To hear with eyes belongs to love's fine wit.

Bearing in mind Shakespeare's evident devotion to Thomas More, it would not be too surprising to believe that he had written a play on the subject of the English Reformation's most famous martyr, whose martyrdom served as the archetype and antetype of all the martyrs to follow, including several whom Shakespeare seems to have known personally.[15]

If Shakespeare is to be taken as the principal author of the play, there remains the question of its unevenness. *Sir Thomas More*, for all its merits and flashes of brilliance, is not of the same quality as other plays that Shakespeare wrote at around the time that the play was submitted to Tilney, such as *Measure for Measure* and *All's Well That Ends Well*, and cannot hold a candle to the works of sheer brilliance, such as *King Lear*, *Othello*, and *Macbeth*, which he would write a couple of years later. Isn't this, in the final reckoning, the biggest single argument against Shakespeare's authorship of the play? Thomas Merriam, who has

---

[15] Further compelling evidence that Shakespeare was well versed in the works of More and that he greatly admired him is provided in the recently published book by Charles and Elaine Hallett, *The Artistic Links between William Shakespeare and Sir Thomas More* (New York: Palgrave Macmillan, 2011).

spent more time than anyone studying the evidence for Shakespeare's involvement with the play, suggests that the play had been written many years earlier, perhaps at the request of his Catholic patron, the Earl of Southampton, or possibly the earl's mother, for private performance at Catholic households.[16] This is entirely possible, considering the tradition of Catholic players performing at the homes of recusant Catholic gentry, and its early date would account for its flaws. As Merriam reminds us, many of Shakespeare's early plays, such as the first and third parts of *Henry VI*, are not masterpieces.[17]

If Merriam is correct, as seems eminently possible, Shakespeare would have known that the play would never be passed by Tilney for performance or publication during the reign of Elizabeth. Perhaps, in the heady and hopeful days following the queen's death, he had dusted off the old play in the hope that the time was ripe for its being approved in the apparently friendly environment of the new king's reign, eliciting the help of fellow playwrights to optimize its chances of acceptance. After all, James' mother, Mary Stuart, had been beheaded on the orders of Elizabeth, as Thomas More had been beheaded on the orders of Elizabeth's father, Henry VIII.

Shakespeare must have had high hopes that the new regime would look kindly on his play. His hopes would be dashed on the rocks as a new wave of brutal persecution hit England's already battered Catholics. Shakespeare would vent his spleen against the new king in the allegorical subplot to *Macbeth* and less obviously but as potently in the other dark plays, such as *Lear* and *Othello*, which reflected the return of darkness to England after the false

---

[16] Thomas Merriam, correspondence with the author, May 11, 2012.
[17] Ibid.

dawn of Elizabeth's death. It would be a further four hundred years, during the reign of another Elizabeth, before *Sir Thomas More* would finally be performed. When the Royal Shakespeare Company staged the play at the new Globe Theatre in the summer of 2005, Shakespeare and More were at last united in art as they had always been in creed. The Bard, who, in Ben Jonson's memorable tribute, "was not of an age, but for all time", had finally been allowed to pay homage to the saint who, in the title of Robert Bolt's memorable play, was "a man for all seasons".